THE SOLIHULL
MANOR HOUSE

AND ITS PEOPLE 1900 *to* 2000

With best wishes.

Fred Ritchie

THE SOLIHULL
MANOR HOUSE

AND ITS PEOPLE 1900 *to* 2000

FRED RITCHIE

BREWIN BOOKS

First published by
Brewin Books Ltd, 56 Alcester Road,
Studley, Warwickshire B80 7LG in 2008
www.brewinbooks.com

ISBN: 978-1-85858-438-6

A Cataloguing in Publication Record
for this title is available from the British Library.

Typeset in Plantin
Printed in Great Britain by
Cromwell Press Ltd.

Contents

Acknowledgments

I owe thanks to the following for contributions given voluntarily or by virtue of their work being copied from archive material held at the Manor House: Rev Robert Pemberton, M.A., Sue Bates, The Solihull News, Cathrina Hulse, Mrs Nancy Andrews, 'St Cyr', Ilse Bell, Christopher Terry, Gwen Bryanston, Pat Lovsey, Julien Reville, Paul Whiston, Susan Owen, Arthur Knowles and David Patterson.

In addition, I should like to acknowledge and thank the following donors for their help, encouragement and input in a variety of ways connected to the research, writing and subsequent illustrating and production of the book. To Pamela May for sorting out the Manor House archives; to all those who took photographs and collected press cuttings and assembled them into a wonderful series of albums kept at the Manor House; to various people who have read my manuscript and provided helpful comments at the editing stage; and to my wife, Pat, for her patience and understanding whilst I 'locked myself away' for the three months I dedicated to writing the story.

Fred Ritchie, March 2008

Author's Notes

When I first considered writing this story, it was because I was moved by the fact that the Manor House had survived virtually intact since 1495. Quite quickly thereafter, I became aware that its survival was entirely dependent upon the people who had lived in it and/or who had loved it.

So the story became a tribute to the countless kind-hearted, dedicated and enthusiastic persons who have cared so tenderly for this beloved old building, particularly over the period since its acquisition by The Solihull Manor House Charity in 1946.

There are a number of devotees who stand head and shoulders above the crowd, not just by virtue of the length of their service to the House, but also by the extent of their enthusiasm and dedication to its safety and well being. Without in any way detracting from the honour which is due to those persons, I feel that there is one who stands out, even amongst the names on that special Roll of Honour. He is Paul Burley. Paul has now notched up thirty six years or so of exceptional service to the Manor House, first as Honorary Architect, subsequently combining that role with membership of the Committee and latterly as its Chairman and also as a Trustee of The Solihull Manor House Charity.

I am of the view that Solihull owes a huge debt of gratitude to Paul Burley for not only helping to save the Manor House in perpetuity for the benefit of the people of Solihull, but for maintaining and improving it with the assistance of countless volunteers and helpers, working alongside a small team of permanent and part time staff.

Fred Ritchie, February 24th 2008

List of Illustrations

Chapter One

Setting the Scene

I have to confess at the very outset, that I do not make any claim to be an historian. At school, history vied with geography to be my least favourite subject. In a way, that serves to underline the intensity of my feelings for The Manor House and the fact that I have been moved to write this short history of the House, albeit limited to events which have occurred there during the 20th century.

My own involvement with the Manor House covers a very short period of time, so I shall be relying upon such records as exist, augmented by personal experiences of some friends and acquaintances whose association with this fine old building goes back, in some cases, as far as the 1920s. Prior to being invited to serve on the Management Committee in October 2005 (as part of an injection of "young blood" – flattering, as I was then in my 70th year!) I, like many other Solihull residents, had been aware of the existence of the Manor House although I had never stepped across the threshold, let alone given any thought to its history.

It would be inappropriate, however, to launch into a series of tales set in the 20th century if I failed to put them into context. To do that I have to go back over five hundred years to 1495, the year, reputedly, in which this family home, eventually to become known as the Manor House, was built. Every time I now cross the threshold of the Manor House, I am reminded that, literally, I am following in the footsteps of people who have done likewise for around five hundred and twenty years. Authentication of the date of construction is difficult if not impossible as records, if they exist at all, are vague. Less contentious is the claim that the House was built for the Greswold (later Greswolde and now Griswold) family.

To further underline the chronological context of the 'birth' of the Manor House, just ten years earlier in 1485, Henry VII, the founder of the Tudor dynasty, ascended the throne of England, following the defeat of Richard III at the Battle of Bosworth. And it was just three years after Christopher Columbus set off, in 1492, on his epic voyage during which he discovered the Americas.

The evidence of ownership by the Greswold family throughout the next four hundred years becomes apparent as one trawls through parish records and the work of genuine historians. With such a wealth of data to hand, it is tempting to veer off the path and start writing about the Greswold family, albeit in the context of the Manor House, forgetting that the objective is to concentrate on the 20th century. The Greswold heirs and successors (the Griswolds), although now resident in America, still retain an active interest in their connections with this part of the world and will, no doubt, have recourse to even more accurate data than I could ever hope to find, so I will steer well clear of that course of action.

Before I do get down to the largely post-Greswold era, let me share this snippet of information with you. In his book "Solihull and its Church", published in 1905 by William Pollard & Co Ltd. of Exeter, the Reverend Robert Pemberton M.A., who titles himself Assistant Curate of Solihull, writes as follows: ....*in a "Survey of the Manor of Solihull, October 14 1629 and April 14 1630" it is listed that "Edward Grissolde, gent, holdeth of the said Lord freely two houses two backsides and three gardens by suit of Court yearly rent 4d."*

I assume that the other house to which reference is made here is the one reputedly built in 1571 by Richard Greswold adjacent to the Manor House, *"possibly as a lodge to the larger house"*, according to Pemberton. He also tells us that in 1905 the property was then a corn store. Today, it can be clearly identified by the inscription on the front wall, "RG 1571 TH 1845." An additional property has been squeezed into the space between it and the Manor House in the intervening years. The "TH" referred to is Thomas Harborne, son of the then churchwarden, Thomas Harborne Senior, who is believed to have lived in the Manor House and who was married to a Greswold.

Strong connections between the Church, the Greswolds and the Manor House crop up elsewhere in Pemberton. In one reference he writes, *"Henry Greswold was Rector of Solihull from 1660 until 1700 when he died."*

The Manor House, circa 1900, by Trinder.

I am also indebted to Pemberton for the following piece of historical information. He writes, *"....the grand old timbered house often called the Manor House"* was located in the High Street *"formerly Smith Street or le Smythe-stret"* in an earlier era. Continuing with his description he says, *"It was built on the Manor, but was never really the Manor House, nor did it ever belong to the Lord of the Manor. It is a magnificent specimen of an old building, and was a very early, if not original seat of the Greswolds in Solihull, and still belongs to that family. Formerly the upper storey projected beyond the lower, but the latter has been brought forward, 2s 6d per annum being paid to the Manor for the encroachment."*

The Reverend Pemberton very neatly sets the scene for the start of my attempt to record some of the more significant events which have occurred to and at the Manor House in the 20th century. I am privileged to have access to title deeds and legal documents tracking specific events involving the property and to Minute books and a range of archive documents which add flesh to those bones.

Chapter Two

1900 to 1945

*"In the High Street remains the Manor House,
really the Greswold family house, a fine pre-Reformation
building with mid-gable, two gables left and right
and a porch gate, a very attractive group."*

The Buildings of England:
"Warwickshire" by Pevsner & Wedgwood, 1966

The Greswolde family connection with the Manor House was set to continue for the first twenty years of the 20th century. It was not until October 28th 1920 that the family finally disposed of its interest in the property, ending some four hundred and twenty five years of ownership. By a conveyance of that date, Francis Wigley Greswolde Greswolde-Williams Esquire passed ownership of the *"freehold land messuage and premises situate in and being known as 'Lime Tree House' High Street Solihull in the County of Warwick"* to Dr Edward Ferdinand Page.

The House, then known as Lime Tree House, took its name from the lime trees planted across the frontage about two hundred years earlier. Contemporary photographs and illustrations of the House all show these lime trees.

Dr Page lived in and ran his surgery from the Manor House for the next sixteen years. I am indebted to local historian Sue Bates for the following extract from an article published in The Solihull News of December 29th 1995, in which she wrote as follows. *"Dr Ferdinand Page was the last person to live at the Manor House. The second of three generations of doctors in the village Ferdinand held his surgery at the Manor House. His father was Edward Sutton*

Page, who held many important medical appointments in Solihull and his son was Erik Page who held his surgery in Herbert Road. The three doctors practised medicine in Solihull for more than 100 years."

I am also indebted to the Solihull News for introducing me to someone with a very personal recollection of Dr Page. A journalist by the name of Cathrina Hulse published an article in the edition of March 31st 2006, in which she echoed my appeal to readers for information about the Manor House. Mrs Nancy Andrews (nee Franklin) of Dorridge, a Life Subscriber to The Manor House Charity, responded to this appeal by calling me on April 5th 2006 to inform me that Dr Page had saved her life in 1924. Then just one year old, Nancy suffered from acute eczema which Dr Page attributed to malnourishment. Following a number of adjustments to her dietary regime, Nancy was soon on the road to full recovery. As a child, living then in Alderbrook Road, Nancy has clear recollections of subsequent attendances at Dr Page's surgery at the Manor House.

It is to Dr Ferdinand Page that we must attribute the change of name of the House from Lime Tree House or The Limes to the Manor House. The conveyance, dated July 17th 1936, by which he passed ownership of and title to the property, to William Edward Wright (later to become Alderman Wright) refers to the property simply as *"The Old Manor House in the High Street Solihull in the County of Warwick."*

It seems unlikely that Mr Wright ever 'moved in' as, just over two months later, on September 26th 1936, he sold the Manor House to Ansells Brewery.

In another article which I unearthed during my research (this one cannot be attributed as it bears no title of the author but is believed to have been written by Miss Flora M. Forster, of whom more will be said later) the following insight is given. *"Ansells, hoping to adapt the house for a country-club hotel, acquired a substantial parcel of land for use as a car park from the owners of the old mansion next door, Messrs Harris Brothers. Difficulties arose about this proposed development, the Second World War broke out and the Manor House stood empty for years until it was used as a local headquarters for the Home Guard."*

This article continues as follows: *"In April 1944, Messrs Ansell announced that the Manor House was to be put up for auction. Mr John Burman, a well known authority on local history and Mr E Orrett, then Headmaster of Sharmans Cross School, were the first to take action; they urged Solihull Urban District*

A photograph of a lovely picture by Arthur Knowles of the rear yard of the Manor House, dated 1951.

Council to buy the house and use it for some public purpose. Mr Burman also secured the promise of several large donations should it become necessary to save the house by public subscription. Messrs Ansell agreed to sell at the price they had given for the house and grounds (plus the extra land acquired from Messrs Harris Brothers) and to also hold up the sale till April 1945. When the Urban District Council refused to buy the Manor House a committee was set up to raise a fund by public subscription. Large scale advertising succeeded in raising the £8,000 required for the purchase price. The next stage was the setting up of the Manor House Trust and its recognition as a charity, whose objects are to preserve the fabric of the house in perpetuity and to use it for the benefit of the people of Solihull."

I have reproduced the above article in full as it serves to sum up, quite succinctly, the content of several other articles dealing with this very important stage in the preservation of the Manor House. In one of those, published in

The News of Saturday 15th February 1958, the author, writing under the pen name of St Cyr, reflects on the part he/she and others played in securing success for the public appeal. *"I had a word with certain prominent advertising people, pressmen and others, and as a result, the campaign became an almost fantastic offensive under the dynamic guidance of D. D. McLachlan, Advertising Manager of Hercules Cycles, closely assisted by 'Jimmy' Stagg, a genius for display, the late Herbert Cater, journalist, and W. T. Bertram, also an advertising man. I became treasurer and never worked so hard in all my life."*

St. Cyr also reveals that the full sum raised by the public subscription appeal was £12,000, £8,000 for the purchase and a further £4,000 to *"put the house into good order."*

The 'public faces' of the appeal included Sir Robert Bland Bird and Lady Bird, Captain Oliver Bird and Stanley Icke, all of whom made generous donations to the fund. St. Cyr informs us, *"Schools and various organisations piled in and in the space of less than one month, the job was done and Solihull's old-world character was saved."*

The culmination of this stage in the transfer of the House from Ansells Brewery was effected by the formation of a charitable trust, The Solihull Manor House Charity, to take over from the appeals committee and to become the new owners of the Manor House. The founding trustees of the Charity were Sir Robert Bland Bird of The White House, Solihull; John Burman of Greenfields, Hampton Lane, Solihull; Flora Macrae Forster of 62a High Street, Solihull (then Headmistress of Solihull High School for Girls); and Roland Charles Lines of Linehurst, Beechnut Lane, Solihull. The members of the appeals committee (described in the Trust Deed as 'the original Committee') included three of the above (Sir Robert Bland Bird is the exception) plus Lady Edith Bird, Mr A. Capon, Mr A. R. Thompson, Mr O. Esmond Kirk, Thomas Rook and one other whose name is illegible. Mr Philip Skelcher, who had been involved in the campaign to save the Manor House, was appointed honorary architect.

Although the Trust Deed of April 6th 1946 defines the above persons as 'the original Committee', in truth they were the people who remained in office as at that date. Mr W. Hand was the inaugural Honorary Treasurer but pressure of work forced his withdrawal at an early stage in the fund-raising process. He was succeeded by Mr E. N. Hiley. Various references are made to Major Cyril R. Parr who had been the officer commanding the Home Guard unit based at the Manor House. Major Parr had developed a deep sense of devotion to the House and sought to do everything in his power to preserve it. He is credited with having guided the process whereby The Solihull Manor House Charity came into being. Countless others also played vital roles in this campaign and to all of them and those listed above, we give thanks for preserving this fine old House in perpetuity for the benefit of the people of Solihull.

April 6th 1946, the date upon which the conveyance of the Manor House from Ansells Brewery Limited to The Solihull Manor House Charity was concluded, marks an important milestone in the life of the building. There appears to be little doubt that if this initiative had never been undertaken or if it had failed, the Manor House would have been demolished to make way for yet another modern retail unit or office block.

Concurrent with the sale of the House and gardens to the Charity, was the transfer of certain pieces of land to the Solihull Corporation. Even after that was taken into account, it is recorded that, at the time of purchase, the grounds of the Manor House were said to *embrace an area of over 3,800 square yards*", (3,177 square metres). See Appendix Five.

A black and white photograph of the Manor House taken around the time of the public appeal in 1945.

Chapter Three

1946 to 1950

The fact that the Manor House was seriously dilapidated and very dirty when it was acquired by the Trustees of The Solihull Manor House Charity is borne out by the following excerpt from a letter I received from a former 'ward' of Flora Macrae Forster, the then Headmistress of Solihull High School for Girls (subsequently Malvern Hall and presently Saint Martin's). Miss Forster gave shelter to a young girl, a refugee from Austria, Ilse Korn, at her home at 62a High Street, Solihull, just a couple of doors up the street from the Manor House (the postal address of which was then 58 High Street). Ilse became a pupil at Solihull High School for Girls and then went on to teach there after graduating from Birmingham University. A local contact gave me Ilse's present address in Norwich.

Ilse wrote as follows: "*What I do remember vividly were the Sunday morning scrubbing sessions at the newly acquired Manor House. My chief job was 'water-carrier'; Miss Forster's flat, in another old house next door (towards the church) was conveniently near to supply hot water for the scrubbing. We put on the bathroom geyser, filled two buckets at a time and conveyed them down the beautiful old staircase, across what is now the little street connecting the High Street and the Mall (I believe) but then was just a drive ending in a ramshackle old garage, into the Manor House, up the staircase to the other girls waiting there with their scrubbing brushes. I think I enjoyed the water-carrying better than the scrubbing! It must have been summer because I remember just wearing a wrap-around overall. It was warm work. The floorboards were anything but smooth and the dirt was well ingrained. I seem to remember that the floor was not even, either. Maybe I was no longer at school, but a student at Birmingham, because I don't think I knew the girls.*"

9

The 'drive ending in a ramshackle old garage' to which Ilse refers is now Manor Walk, connecting the High Street with Manor Square and the eastern entrance to Touchwood Shopping Centre.

Immediately post World War II, Community Associations were being set up across Great Britain. These were social and cultural organisations whose objectives were the provision of educational and recreational activities to facilitate the rebuilding of communities following the end of hostilities and the demobilisation of service personnel. The Education Act of 1944 afforded financial support for these Associations. The Manor House Committee actively supported the formation of such an Association in Solihull and saw it as being an ideal organisation to take over occupancy of the Manor House. They shared a common objective which was to provide services and facilities *'for the benefit of the people of Solihull.'*

Miss Forster, in a note, undated but probably prepared in 1959 or 1960, informs us that, *"On the initiative of Major Parr, the Solihull Community Association was formed, Mr A. R. Thompson, Headmaster of Solihull School, became its first Chairman........."* In a further note prepared by Miss Forster in December 1965, she informs us that the Solihull Community Association was launched *"at a big money-raising fête held at Tudor Grange in 1946. Mr P. F. Glendon, as its Chairman, gave unstinted (sic) voluntary service to the Manor House for twelve years until his retirement in 1960."*

In her report to the 2nd Annual General Meeting of The Solihull Manor House Trust held on December 8th 1947, Miss Forster writes, *"A five-year repairing lease of the Manor House was granted from January 1st 1947, to the Community Association, on the understanding that the cost of urgent repairs would be met out of the Manor House Fund. The severe winter and other difficulties hindered progress, but since September the Community Association has been functioning in the Manor House. The house was re-wired and minor repairs were undertaken. In all, four rooms have been repaired and re-decorated. The air-raid shelters in the garden were removed in July by the Urban District Council and in October, part of the garden was cleared of rough shrubs, brambles, etc."*

The first room, capable of holding 30 persons, would have been ready for use on or about August 1st 1947. The published hire fee for this room was 5/– (25p) for three hours (summer time) and 7/– (35p) for three hours (winter rate).

SOLIHULL COMMUNITY ASSOCIATION

Chairman	A. R. THOMPSON, Esq., M.A.
Vice-Chairman	MRS. EVANS
Honorary Secretary	J. W. WALL, Esq.
	"Wenlock," School Lane, Solihull
Honorary Treasurer	S. H. SHIPWAY, Esq.

Committee :—

W. E. BENNETT, Esq. (Solihull Unionist Association)
Mrs. G. CHRIST (Red Cross)
P. F. GLENDON, Esq. (Anglo-Soviet Unity Committee)
R. C. LINES, Esq. (Solihull Society of Arts)
A. L. METCALF, Esq. (A.F.S. Association)
V. A. RAINIER, Esq. (Solihull Residents' Association)
J. RICHARDSON, Esq. (British Legion)
Miss F. M. FORSTER, M.A. (representing Manor House Trustees)
JOHN BURMAN, Esq., J.P.   „   „   „   „

Honorary Adviser .... ARTHUR S. DAVIES, Esq.
(Birmingham Council for Community Associations

AFFILIATED ORGANISATIONS :

SOLIHULL SOCIETY OF ARTS	SOLIHULL PHOTOGRAPHIC SOCIETY
BRITISH RED CROSS	SOLIHULL BRITISH RED CROSS
SOLIHULL BEEKEEPERS' ASSOCIATION	SOLIHULL & DISTRICT BRITISH-SOVIET UNITY
SOLIHULL GIRL GUIDES PARENTS' ASSN.	COMMITTEE
SOLIHULL CRICKET & TENNIS CLUB	SOLIHULL BOY SCOUTS PARENTS' ASSOCIATION
SOLIHULL CONSERVATIVE & UNIONIST ASSN.	SOLIHULL BRITISH LEGION
CHAMBER OF TRADE	SOLIHULL COMMUNIST PARTY
G.T.C., SOLIHULL ADVISORY COUNCIL.	SOLIHULL HOME GUARD ASSOCIATION
SOLIHULL DIVISION LIBERAL ASSOCIATION	SOLIHULL HORTICULTURAL SOCIETY
SOLIHULL FIRE SERVICE ASSOCIATION	ELMDON HEATH LABOUR PARTY
MANOR HOUSE PRESERVATION COMMITTEE	QUEEN ELIZABETH HOSPITAL LINEN LEAGUE
U.N.A. SOLIHULL.	REDLANDS SOCIAL CLUB

Solihull Community Association.

Correspondence on file shows that the Community Association initiated and paid for much of the internal repair work during the three and a half years leading up to the granting of a ten year lease on the building in 1950. The terms of this lease, bestowed upon the Community Association responsibility for internal repairs and decoration, whilst the Manor House Committee carried responsibility for all external renovations and repairs. The Minutes of the 1948 AGM contains a snippet of information underlining this sharing of responsibilities in a reference to "*the extension of the chess-room by the removal of the bath-room partition*", which indicates that social activities were by then well established within the House. I understand that what was then "the chess room" is today designated as Room 3, The Pickering Room, on the first floor, occupied by Electric Lemon Limited. The records show that the Solihull Community Association was eventually granted a ten year lease by the Manor House Committee, commencing in June 1950.

Another helpful contact with early memories of those formative days in the life of the 'newly-saved' Manor House was Christopher Terry. As a respondent to my press appeal on March 31st 2006 for information about the Manor House, Chris followed up our telephone conversation with a note containing *"some recollections."* This is what he wrote in part: *"As I remember, Solihull Branch of Toc H was the first organisation to meet in the Manor House on a regular basis, as part of the Community Centre, after it was brought into use after the end of the war. The date was probably 1948–49, but I am not too certain about this. The house was in a deplorable state and Solihull Toc H carried out its own renovations and decorations to Room 6. The Branch was in a flourishing state in the 1950s boasting a membership of up to 35. A regular member, who lived close to the Manor House, made it his job to light the fire before the meeting started at 8.0 o'clock and a fine blaze greeted members as they arrived in the winter months."*

This Booklet Contains
VIEWS OF . . . .
BYGONE SOLIHULL
which will be a treasured
possession in years to come.

The Manor House and Community Centre Fete

TUDOR GRANGE   -   -   -   -   SOLIHULL

SATURDAY   -   -   AUGUST 17th, 1946   -   -   2-30 p.m. to Dusk

THE PAST SALUTES THE FUTURE   1311

Souvenir Programme – The Manor House and Community Centre Fete 1946.

Chapter Four

1950 to 1960

The scene was set for the immediate future of the Manor House. The Solihull Community Association was set to play a vital role in the positioning of the Manor House in the life of Solihull and its inhabitants throughout the fifties. At the time of the granting of the lease, the key players in the Solihull Community Association were as follows:

The Chairman was P. F. Glendon, Esq.; Miss Flora M. Forster, M.A., was the Deputy Chairman; W. E. Bennett, Esq., was Honorary Secretary, the Honorary Treasurer was T. B. Lumb Esq., and P. F. E. Smith, Esq., was Honorary House Secretary. The Executive Committee comprised W. G. Lines, Esq., Mrs M. Matthews, P. J. B. Morgan, Esq., J. H. Richardson, Esq., Miss K. M. Thornton, J. W. Wall, Esq., and E. W. Winckle, Esq. Miss Mildred Scott had been appointed Warden and J. Wood Massey Esq., and Philip Skelcher were, respectively, Honorary Auditor and Architect.

In 1949–50 there were already over forty community organisations affiliated to the Community Association. They embraced art, culture, sport, politics and leisure pursuits and attracted persons of all ages. They vied for use of the available space in the Manor House and as rooms were refurbished and brought into use, the list continued to expand. In an appendix to this short history, I have recorded the names of these organisations.

There is ample evidence that there was a 'joined at the hip' sort of relationship between lessor and lessee throughout the tenure of the Solihull Community Association's occupancy of the Manor House. Several members of the management team of the Community Association were invited year on year to serve on the Management Committee of the Manor House and vice versa. Not once during my research of the records covering this period did I find reference to any sort of stand-off or suggestion that there might be a conflict of interest. On the contrary, there is ample evidence that the Solihull Community Association invested heavily in the refurbishment and upgrading of the accommodation during its thirteen year occupancy of the building. Nor did that generosity end with the expiry of the lease in June 1960. An interest free loan to the Manor House Committee was granted by the Community Association in 1960. This was followed up by a gift of £1,000 in July 1963 *"towards improvements and/or additions to the Manor House to commemorate the work done by the (Solihull) Community Association during its ten year lease of the house."*

Perhaps the relationship between the two bodies is best summed up by quoting the words of Miss Flora Macrae Forster, Honorary Secretary, extracted from the Minutes of the AGM of The Solihull Manor House Charity held on June 23rd 1960, just seven days before the expiry of the Community Association's lease. *"We are grateful to the Community Association and in particular its Chairman, Mr Glendon, for the work they have done during the last thirteen years, in running the house for the benefit of the people of Solihull. Change is now inevitable. We look forward with hope and confidence to the next stage in the life of the old house."*

But I am racing ahead of myself. Back on March 10th 1953, the Honorary Architect, Philip Skelcher, submitted a report to the Management Committee of the Manor House in which he catalogued a depressingly long list of structural work which required urgent attention. Amongst other defects he listed loose brickwork, flaking paintwork, chimney brickwork in poor condition, the rear elevation of the eastern gable showed cracks in the brickwork requiring it to be supported by a buttress wall (or walls), and so on.

Although most of the above could be considered to be relatively urgent, shortage of funds determined that some of it would have to wait and it was not until May 29th 1958 that approval was given to construct *"brick piers against inner side of East Wing"*, the work to be undertaken by Messrs Deebanks against their estimate of £49.15.0.

Two major issues were occupying the minds of the Manor House Committee around this time. A great deal of thought was being given to the possibility and the practicability of building a performance hall in the

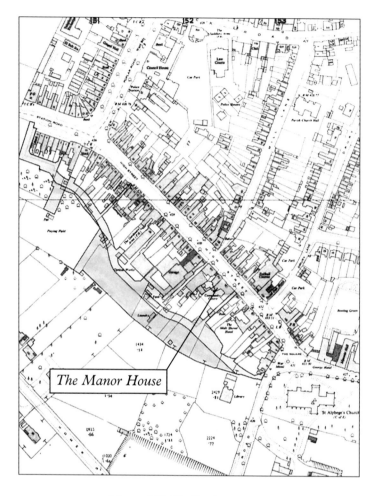

Map of Solihull, circa 1954.

grounds at the rear of the House, capable of seating up to three hundred persons and of staging a variety of events of interest to the local community. Running in parallel with this was the need to address the implications of the compulsory purchase order served on The Solihull Manor House Charity in 1956 in respect of part of the grounds at the rear of the Manor House to accommodate the construction of an access road and a public car park running along the back of the buildings on the south side of the High Street.

The compulsory purchase order negotiations rumbled on for some considerable time and eventually extended to the acquisition by the Council of the driveway leading from the High Street along the eastern side of the Manor House to the old garage, plus some additional ground upon which were to be constructed public conveniences. The area in question appears to have been of the order of 2,640 square yards and the price £1,500. This finally put paid to there being any prospect of building the proposed performance hall. Prolonged negotiations were finally concluded in 1962 by which time the Council had agreed to increase its offer to £2,500 and to build a 6' high wall along the eastern and southern boundaries of what would be the new gardens, inserting a pedestrian gate in the eastern wall, a vehicular access on the southern wall and laying a tarmac drive from the new rear access road in to the Manor House garage.

A further distraction in the late fifties was caused by a proposal to merge the Society of Arts and the Community Association with the former assuming the role of lessee either for the balance of the term of the then existing lease or a new lease for a longer period. The negotiations foundered once it became apparent that the Society of Arts really wanted to purchase the Manor House and to broaden its use, possibly to include the sale of alcohol. I was surprised to read in the Minutes of a Committee meeting held on May 29th 1958 "*That the conveyance of the property from Ansells to The Manor House Trustees contains an absolute prohibition of the sale of intoxicants.*" Once this information was passed to the Society of Arts along with an absolute refusal to even consider the sale of the property (also forbidden by the Trust Deed), the Society of Arts lost all interest in the proposed merger with the Community Association.

In the second paragraph of this chapter, I referred to the struggle by various community groups to find space at the Manor House in the forties and fifties. Gwen Bryanston, a Life Member of The Solihull Manor House Charity, brought this home to me in graphic style in an exchange of emails in July/August 2006. Gwen wrote, "*The Solihull Film Society, now nearly fifty years old, started with a meeting in the Manor House in 1958, when so many people crowded up the stairs to the largest of the rooms that many simply had to be turned away. The Solihull News reported that there were at least seventy people. There was no thought in those days for the fragility of such an ancient building! We showed the film 'Brief Encounter' – and handed a hat around for donations to help us to start the Film Society – which, as you may be aware, still has a large membership and often fills the Library Theatre to full capacity with its monthly shows. My late husband, Mario Bryanston, founded the Film Society and remained its Chairman to within a couple of years of his death."*

Continuing on the theme of the diverse range of community groups using the Manor House at that time, a respondent to my press appeal in March 2006 for information about the House's past, contacted me to tell me she used to attend the Scottish Presbyterian Church meetings which were held there. It turned out that my informant, Mrs Pat Lovsey, was the daughter-in-law of my Showell Green Lane landlady who took me in when I first came to live in Birmingham in 1960/61.

The Manor House Committee suffered a major financial crisis in 1959 when dry rot was discovered in the floor of what was then called the Red Cross Room (Room 7 and currently occupied by Scent to Go). The cost of ripping out all the flooring, skirting etc., and replacing it with a 4 inch deep concrete base overlaid with 1½ inches of pitchmastic flooring nearly cleaned out the small financial reserve which had been slowly accumulating.

With the end of the Community Association's lease looming (June 1960) and strong signals that it would not be interested in seeking an extension in view of the changing nature of the interests and pursuits of the community, the Manor House Committee turned its attention at the turn of the decade, to the post Community Association era. At the 1959 AGM, held on December 18th, it was decided to form a House Management Sub Committee and to appoint a Warden to carry on all of the duties hitherto undertaken by the Community Association. The Manor House Committee was tasked with the need to deal with these detailed plans, which it did at its first meeting in the sixties.

Another era in the life of the Manor House was about to begin.

Chapter Five

The Sixties

In anticipation of the Community Association lease terminating on the 30th of June 1960, the Manor House Committee met on January 22nd of that year to consider the future management and running of the building. It was determined that a Warden should be appointed and that he/she should report to a House Management Sub Committee which, in turn, would report to the Manor House Committee. Mr Percival F. Glendon, then Chairman of the Solihull Community Association, was approached and agreed to act as the temporary Warden to cover the transitional period from April 1st until October 1st 1960. A permanent successor, Mr J. H. Reece, was appointed and assumed the Warden's duties with effect from October 1st.

The House Management Sub Committee, at its first meeting prior to June 30th, elected Councillor J. William (Bill) Wall as its Chairman, Mr Burton Wood as Vice Chairman, and Dennis Gray and Eric Dinwiddie as Honorary Secretary and Honorary Treasurer, respectively. Agreement was reached with regard to the sharing of responsibilities for the running and management of the House along very similar lines to those which had obtained throughout the period of tenure of the Solihull Community Association.

There were at that time around forty organisations and associations, mostly affiliated to the Community Association, which were using the Manor House for meetings, functions and social occasions. With that level of usage established, the Manor House Committee could turn its attention to a concern which it had about the long term future of the Charity. The wording of the original Trust Deed of April 6th 1946 required to be amended to enable the Charity to look forward with confidence to this new future which had just dawned. At a Special General Meeting of the Charity held on March

17th 1961, amendments to the Trust Deed were adopted to give effect to (a) the introduction of a category of Life Subscribers to the Charity upon payment of a single fee of £5 and Annual Subscribers upon payment of the sum of five shillings (25p); (b) the right to co-opt new Trustees; (c) the requirement that the Hon Secretary and Treasurer plus one third of the ordinary members of the Committee should retire by rotation, but with the opportunity to stand for re-election; and (d) the right to co-opt non-subscribers to serve on the Committee but not to VOTE! The Supplemental Deed which gave effect to these changes was finally engrossed on October 26th 1962.

This proved to be the first of several such documents. Indeed, by the time I assumed the role of Honorary Secretary in 2006, two further Deeds of Variation had been incorporated, one dated November 25th 1993 and the other September 22nd 1997. By this stage the Trust Deed had become so complex that it was virtually impossible to tell whether or not the Committee was functioning within the terms of its mandate. One of the first tasks I set myself was the production of one single document which incorporated all of the many amendments made over the previous sixty years. A couple of shortcomings were thrown up by this action, as a result of which a further Deed of Variation was prepared, approved at a General Meeting of the Charity and passed into law on June 26th 2007.

On a lighter note and one which made me smile, particularly given the present climate of health and safety issues relating to tasks undertaken by schoolchildren making such an event an absolute non-starter, was the recording in the Minutes of the Manor House Committee meeting of 15th November 1961 to the effect that, "*Miss Griffiths had arranged for young helpers from Malvern Hall to snowcem the back of the house....*" Such was the pressure on available funds and the community spirit which then prevailed, that this would have been regarded as absolutely the right thing to do in the circumstances.

It was around this time that Miss Flora Macrae Forster "parted" from Malvern Hall. Nothing further is recorded to amplify the meaning and interpretation of the word "parted" but one can only assume that she retired from her post as Head of the School and that it had nothing to do with pupils being used to snowcem the back of the Manor House!

The Manor House became the beneficiary of one or two very attractive relics in 1962. Just prior to the demolition of Touchwood Hall in 1963 the Solihull Borough Council gifted a carved oak chimney piece and an ornate shell-headed cupboard, as well as a quantity of original floorboards and at least one door, all salvaged from the Hall.

The chimney piece was installed in the main entrance hall where it remains to this day. There is some speculation as to what existed there before. It would appear that the original hearth stretched back to the wall of the Kirk Room. Step inside the hearth today and you will see that a dividing wall has been inserted to reduce by more than half this original grate cavity.

As to the shell-headed cupboard, this can be seen today where it is installed in the west wall of the Kirk Room. It would appear that this was not its original location as, after much consideration, the Manor House Committee authorised the Warden to issue an instruction to the builder (Mr Deebank) around September 1962 to cover, "..*building in the shell cupboard on the landing; and also to ask him to salvage more floorboards from Touchwood Hall,*" amongst other things.

There was obviously a need to review the emergency escape procedures at this time, resulting in a fire escape being installed in the east wing (it remains there today) and a further door being cut through the wall between Rooms 4 and Room 5 to provide an alternative means of escape. The work was carried out by the Midland Fire Equipment Company at a cost of £241.00. The door salvaged from Touchwood Hall and mentioned above was installed between Rooms 4 and 5. I believe that it was subsequently replaced as it was neither fire nor sound proof.

Tragedy struck early in 1963 with the sudden death of Mr Oliver Esmond Kirk, Chairman of the Manor House Committee. The Minutes of the AGM of the Charity held on July 10th record the following tribute paid to Mr Kirk. "*Miss Griffiths (the Assistant Honorary Secretary) opened her report with a tribute to the late Chairman, Mr Esmond Kirk, whose sudden death on February 22nd had been a great loss to his family and friends and to the Manor House Committee, as well as to a wider circle. His integrity, his enthusiasm, his gentleness and humour and the wisdom distilled from a wide experience had made up a rare personality.*"

The election of his widow, Mrs Barbara Kirk, to fill the vacant post of Chairman received the unanimous support of the Manor House Committee when it met on March 13th 1963. Mrs Kirk remained in this post until 1978. She continued to serve on the Committee into the early eighties, a continuous period of dedicated service exceeding thirty years. The combined period of service given by Mr and Mrs Kirk in support of the Charity exceeded fifty years. It is therefore little wonder that a room in the Manor House was dedicated as The Kirk Room in recognition of their combined contribution. And so it remains to this day. The Kirk Room can be found on the ground floor, east wing, facing on to the High Street.

The tradition of naming a room in the Manor House has continued down the decades, the latest such dedication being to the memory of Molly Bullock in 2007. The problem facing future generations is that there are insufficient rooms left unnamed to cater for the ever-lengthening list of dedicated voluntary workers who have given years and years of service to the Charity.

By 1964 the list of organisations, clubs and societies which regularly used the Manor House had risen to between seventy and eighty. Space was at a premium and support services were stretched in an effort to cope. A decision was taken to add a further room at the back of the east wing and to provide a covered way along the back of the building to facilitate movement between the different parts of the building. The new room, named the Glendon Room in honour of Mr Percival F. Glendon, was officially opened on January 16th 1965 by the Mayor and Mayoress of Solihull, Councillor and Mrs Harold Charles Taylor.

The covered walkway still exists but the Glendon Room had to be removed to make way for the addition of the Manor House Tea Room (the Burley Room) which was constructed in 2004.

In January 1966 the Manor House Committee was approached by developers who were in the process of replacing the old building next door at 124 High Street, formerly occupied by Hull, the butcher, with a new retail unit which would become Peter's Bookshop. They had discovered a large protrusion on the ground floor party wall shared with the Manor House. It turned out to be the back of a very deep oven on the western wall of the old kitchen (the Joyce Griffiths Room or Griff Room as it is more frequently called) on the ground floor. This oven was some seven feet deep, most of which jutted through the wall into what would have originally been the land between the Manor House and the building constructed by Richard Greswold in 1571 (see Chapter One for further information). The drawing of the new retail unit prepared by J. Seymour

Harris & Partners in January 1966 shows the 'carbuncle' and the proposal to remove it flush with the boundary wall. By September of that year, demolition at 124 High Street had been completed and the west wall of the Manor House had been shored up with five buttresses. Negotiations rumbled on for some months; special consideration had to be given to alterations to an ancient building; the Charity Commission had to be consulted; Solihull Borough Council's approval had to be sought; and there was the matter of compensation to be considered. By the time all of these matters had been concluded in December 1966, construction work on the site at 124 High Street was well under way. The Manor House Committee had accepted an offer of £300 in compensation for the loss of the back of the oven, the builders had agreed to brick up the wall where the oven had protruded through it and also to carry out repairs to the guttering at the front of the House over Room 5 which had been damaged during demolition of the old building at 124 High Street.

The Minutes record the beginnings of rumblings of discontent between the members of the House Management Sub Committee and the Manor House Committee in the summer of 1967. It had obviously become difficult to distinguish between the activities and responsibilities of the two committees resulting in a certain amount of treading upon each other's toes. At a joint meeting of the two groups on September 20th, but only after some sharp exchanges, Councillor Carter proposed, *"That this joint meeting approves in principle the merging of the Manor House Committee and the House Management Sub Committee, with co-options as necessary."* The motion was carried unanimously.

Thanks were due in no small part to the groundwork done by the Solihull Community Association in the fifties, for the healthy calendar of activities taking place at the Manor House as the sixties drew to a close. I have to declare a personal interest in one of the groups which met there regularly from 1967 although I cannot claim to have been a member at that time. The Solihull Writers' Workshop was established in 1967 by Nora Rock and Roma Grover and originally met at the Manor House. Many years later I joined the SWW, when I first became interested in writing. By this time the group was meeting at the Margaret Wharam Room of the Methodist Church by Solihull Station, on the second and fourth Wednesdays of each month, commencing at 7.30pm. I was made most welcome, as are all new members. But I digress. Back to the Solihull Manor House and on to the seventies!

Chapter Six

The Seventies

The House was obviously being very heavily used by the turn of the sixties/seventies. I found a file belonging to the then Warden, Mrs Miller, containing correspondence from a vast number of societies, organisations and others, relating to bookings being made for the year 1976. As I thought that this may prove to be quite evocative, I have prepared a list of the names of the correspondents (see Appendix Two). No doubt there were other users who made verbal bookings so this list cannot be taken as being either definitive or exhaustive, but it does give some indication of the footfall through the building at that time. With the benefit of hindsight, one has to ask whether or not such intensive use of an ancient building was sensible. It is a consideration which confronts the Manor House Committee of today when it is trying to set a balance between under and over-utilisation of the House.

As an illustration of not only the number of people passing through the House, but the diversity of the use to which it was being put at that time, I will try to recall a conversation I had with a Rotarian friend of many years standing, Sam Ichbia. Sam told me that prior to the construction of the Synagogue in Monastery Drive in the late seventies, the Solihull and District Hebrew Congregation met at a number of venues including the Manor House. The SDHC, formed in 1963, had embraced some fifty families by the seventies and could attract a congregation of anything up to one hundred at special religious festivals such as Yom Kippur and Rosh Hashanah. The Garwood Room was the only room big enough to accommodate the SDHC. Sam had the task of carrying in the Ark, which he brought in the back of his Volvo, on a Friday evening, so that everything could be set up prior to the Sabbath. Apparently a desk, half of a wardrobe and some curtains completed the ceremonial altar upon which were placed the Scrolls. Sam recalls that the SDHC was warmly received and made to feel most welcome by the Manor House staff.

There is an air of austerity pervading the written records maintained during the early part of the seventies. It is evident to the reader that funds were limited and that the House and its contents were in constant need of repair and attention. In the Minutes of the September 1972 meeting of the Committee there is reference to the fact that repairs to the roof had been completed but that it had only been possible to carry out the work thanks to a grant from Solihull Council.

The merger of the House Management Sub Committee and the Manor House Committee, to which I made reference towards the close of the last chapter, had obviously been completed as there were ten attendees at this September meeting and twelve apologies! Of the ten attendees, seven were ladies, and of the twelve absentees, eight were ladies. Where would the Manor House have been without the voluntary work which was being done by the ladies. It was around this time that I found the first reference to an Executive Committee. Having resolved the late sixties problem of duplication, another would appear to have been put in its place.

As part of the battle to raise sufficient funds to cover ever-increasing expenditure in the early part of the decade, Group Membership was created to run alongside the group of supporters called "The Friends of the Manor House." This was targeted at the large number of organisations and bodies which were using rooms at the Manor House. The fact that these organisations would be able to send a nominee to attend the annual general meetings of The Solihull Manor House Charity if they became a Group Member proved to be insufficient to attract a large number of them to subscribe, even at £1 per annum, so the scheme failed to contribute the sums needed to swell the funds.

An extensive redecorating programme was carried out in the years leading up to the mid-seventies. The available funds would not stretch to employing professionals to carry out this work so it was done, in the main, by volunteers! Groups of up to ten "Friends" and members of the Committee would turn up at weekends, armed with paint brushes and would get stuck in. There is something about the House which evokes this sort of spirit amongst its supporters. Another reference in the records struck a chord with me. Ray Pope, of whom more will be said later, is reported as having *"compiled a leaflet giving a brief history of the Manor House"* in 1974. Is that where I got my inspiration? He was obviously more confident about attracting mass readership with his work than I am about mine. Ray had 3,500 copies of his leaflet printed! So far, I have been unable to trace a single copy so they obviously proved to be popular. There may be hope for my efforts yet!

One essential piece of expenditure which had to be undertaken within the limited reserves available (and conserved by the efforts of the above volunteers) was the provision, in 1974, of a new metal fire escape with chequered plates (steps, I assume) to replace the old one which was fitted with wooden steps! Not much use in a fire, so it is easy to comprehend the urgency of installing the replacement. To galvanise or not to galvanise, that was the question. In the end the Committee, swayed by financial considerations, decided against galvanisation, accepting that the stair would have to have a good coat of paint from time to time but that was an expenditure which could be deferred until a later date.

The second half of the seventies appears to have been slightly less financially fraught for the Manor House Committee. This is due in no small part to the activities of the "Ladies' Committee." This appears to have evolved rather than to have been constitutionally commissioned. That there were tensions between the Ladies' Committee and the Manor House Committee is not in doubt but the former was doing such a great job in helping to (or actually) running the House that it was left to get on with it for the main part. Significant sums of money were raised from the staging of an impressive programme of events organised by the Ladies' Committee and this was then put to excellent use in refurbishing such as the kitchen with new appliances, some of the rooms with new curtains and floor-coverings, as well as maintaining an on-going programme of redecoration. Even the garden came in for a bit of attention around this time. Dr Elisabeth Scull told me she joined the Committee in the mid 60s, having been proposed by Miss Forster. Elisabeth Hardeman as she was at this time, had little interest in the running of the house so she teamed up with Joyce Griffiths ("Griff") and together they started to knock the grounds into shape, a task which was to occupy her for the next twenty years.

Julien Reville, Director of Electric Lemon Limited, the company which currently occupies Room 3 (The Pickering Room), has fond recollections of the latter part of the seventies. Julien is a bit of a thespian in his leisure time and in the seventies he was a regular member of "The Numeriques", which rehearsed at the Manor House under the direction of Brenda Rolfe.

Early in 1976, the Community Health Service took a three year licence on a room at the Manor House. Although the records are unclear as to exactly which room it occupied, it would appear to have been Room 5, which is at the front of the House, on the first floor of the west wing. Such a regular and reliable source of income would have proved to be very attractive to the Committee and at the same time it had the effect of reducing the footfall and the dependence upon casual lettings.

There is a very touching reference in the minutes of a meeting of the Committee held early in 1977, when the Chairman, Mrs Barbara Kirk presented the Warden, Mrs Phyllis Miller with a small gift to mark Mrs Miller's twenty-five year period of service at the Manor House. Mrs Miller joined the team in 1952, became Deputy Warden in 1962 and Warden in 1972. Little did Mrs Kirk know then, but Mrs Miller was due to carry on for another eleven years.

Mrs Miller; Ray Pope; Stella Wright; Margaret O'Dell; and Pamela May.

Staying with the subject of tributes, Barbara Kirk was about to be on the receiving end of one herself, when she declined to stand for re-election as Chairman of the Committee following the 1977 Annual General Meeting of The Solihull Manor House Charity. By this time Barbara Kirk had served as Chairman for fourteen years and had been a member of the Committee since 1949. This is an extract from the Minutes of a meeting held on June 28th 1977. "*Mr Greenwood (on behalf of the Committee) paid tribute to all her work and devotion to the House, also to that of her late husband. They had made the House part of our community, maintained standards and helped to make the House what it is today.*" Mr Dinwiddie then added the following, "*She was tactful, diplomatic and never ruffled and that we had been exceedingly fortunate in knowing both Mrs Kirk and her late husband.*" To

further underline these tributes, the Committee then declared its intention to name Room 1 "The Esmond and Barbara Kirk Room" as a permanent thank you to Mr and Mrs Kirk. By the time the Committee got around to commissioning the brass plate for the door of Room 1, it had decided to shorten the name to "The Kirk Room", and so it remains to this day.

Raymond (Ray) Charles Pope, who had joined the Committee in 1975, was elected to serve as Chairman following the 1977 AGM. He was to remain in this post until 1986.

In the latter part of 1977, it became necessary to examine the exterior black and white decoration of the High Street frontage, where peeling paintwork was allowing rainwater to penetrate between the timbers. In November, contractors were called in to sandblast the façade to

Going, going, gone.....

determine the extent of the problem. Scaffolding had been erected and enclosed by tarpaulins to prevent injury or distress to pedestrians using the High Street. On November 7th, exceedingly high winds blew the entire structure down, tearing the rainwater pipes off the front of the House and demolishing a street lamp. Thankfully, no one was injured.

The investigative work was completed; it was clear that major restoration work would prove to be necessary. The Committee would have to determine how and when this would be carried out and more importantly, how it could be funded.

1977 closed with the planting, on November 26th, of a maple tree, presented by the Horticultural Society, to commemorate the Silver Jubilee of Her Majesty Queen Elizabeth's accession to the throne. Just prior to that event, Charles Lines had offered to write a booklet about the Manor House and had invited Paul Burley, then Honorary Architect to the Charity, to do illustrations. The only slightly downbeat item of any significance was the need to remove a chimney which had developed a list and was in danger of collapsing. This latter project became quite protracted due to the need to close Manor Walk for safety reasons, thus restricting the work to Sundays. It was finally completed early in 1978.

As I read through the various records covering the closing years of this decade, I could almost feel the energy which had been driving the Committee forward through 1976 and 1977. This 'power surge' resulted in what can only be described as a very brave act given the Charity's financial circumstances which prevailed at the time. In the spring of 1978, the Committee commissioned the restoration programme, primarily to the façade of the House, estimated to cost up to £20,000. The grit-blasting of the frontage of the House, which had been undertaken in November 1977 when the scaffolding collapsed, had revealed "*a state of repair better than feared but worse than hoped for*", according to the wording of a Restoration Public Appeal for funding issued on April 8th 1978. The wording of the appeal continues as follows, "*A number of oak rails and studs need replacement, others need repairs; eighty wattle and daub infill panels require repairs or replacement; one window casement is beyond repair; a number of bricks are disintegrating and the brickwork needs repointing. The repairs and restoration are considered vital and urgent.*"

Although submissions to both West Midlands County Council and Solihull Metropolitan Borough Council for grants and/or loans to help to cover the cost of this work had been put in motion, the selected contractor, Sapcotes, was commissioned to commence work prior to the Committee receiving any reply to these applications. A bank loan was negotiated to cover the cost of the contract and as a safety net, the above £22,000 fund raising appeal was launched. Extended payment terms had also been offered by Sapcotes, but even given all those 'safeguards', the situation remained somewhat precarious for some time.

Good fortune smiled upon the Committee. West Midlands County Council was the first to come on board with an offer of a £5,000 grant in May 1978. As the restoration work progressed, dry rot was discovered in the floorboards in the Kirk Room. This would add a further £1,000 or thereabouts to the final bill. In August, SMBC came up with an interest free loan repayable in two years' time which was sufficient to cover the balance of the cost of the project. Meanwhile, the public appeal and the Committee's own fund raising activities were generating a creditable inflow of funds. It took five months to complete the restoration programme and the final bill was nudging up towards the originally estimated cost of £20,000. By this time the funding crisis had passed and the Committee was confident that the bill could be paid, loans discharged and that there would still be a credit balance at the bank.

In 1979, the re-wiring of the House proved to be necessary so another £2,264 + VAT had to be found and an act of vandalism was recorded in July of that year, when three window panes at the front of the House were smashed.

The seventies closed to mixed reviews. The Red Cross had signed a new three year licence on Room 7 but the Citizens Advice Bureau had given notice that it would be quitting the House at the end of October. New community groups were still being formed, one being the Solihull Young National Trust, the inaugural meeting of which was held on October 9th 1979 in the Glendon Room. With the objective of encouraging the interest and involvement of young persons (16–25 years) in conservation, fund raising and voluntary work for the National Trust, the Solihull Manor House must have proved itself to be an ideal venue. I am grateful to founder member, Susan Owen (nee Monks) for this emailed contribution which continues as follows:

Restoration Appeal Leaflet.

"*Monthly evening meetings were held at the Manor House when visiting speakers would talk to us about their work or hobby. Some of the subjects of the early meetings were Midland Wind and Water Mills, Restoration of Church Bells, and Restoration work at Baddesley Clinton – following acquisition by the National Trust.*"

The Committee had found it necessary to review room hire charges to meet ever increasing overheads and the decade closed with rumblings of discontent being voiced by societies and organisations which had been using the House over many years. Requests for loyalty and regular user discounts had to be declined by the Committee, resulting in some uncertainty about the future level of usage of rooms available for regular and casual bookings. Altogether, an unsettling conclusion to another decade of achievement by the Manor House team.

Chapter Seven

1980 to 1983

Τhis was the beginning of a decade during which stress would be a significant factor in the life of both the Manor House and the people who were running it. Despite the fact that the House was being heavily, perhaps even over utilised, it was proving difficult to generate enough revenue from lettings and other activities to keep up with the constant demands placed upon the funds to meet bills for maintenance and restoration work. The pressure on the paid and voluntary staff appears to have caused some friction from time to time, bringing about changes in personnel and working practices and even rubbing off on users of the House on occasions.

Despite the foregoing, 1980 started on a high with the completion of a three year licence by the Community Health Council on Room 5. Negotiations had been rumbling on for almost a year by this time; the previous licence had expired in March 1979. The Community Health Council was the new title of the former Community Health Service which had first taken up residence back in 1976.

To add to the problems mentioned in the opening paragraph, vandalism became a regular occurrence in the High Street around this time. The House came under attack, windows were broken from time to time and staff members were being subjected to abuse. Roaring inflation, up at around 20% in 1980, merely added to the overall problems associated with running the Manor House.

The date was looming by which repayment had to be made of the loan of £16,000 from Solihull Metropolitan Borough Council to assist with the restoration programme carried out in 1978. Despite the enormous success of the public appeal and the fund-raising activities of the voluntary workers and staff at the Manor House, it was evident that the loan could not be discharged in full without placing the Manor House Committee's finances in a precarious position. A compromise was reached with SMBC; £14k was repaid in September 1980 and repayment of the balance was deferred until 1982.

1980 was to end on a sad note. Miss Flora Macrae Forster, a founder Trustee, Honorary Secretary from 1946 until 1969 and a member of the Committee until 1973, intimated that she wished to stand down as a Trustee, severing her last link with The Solihull Manor House Charity. After thirty-five years of exceptionally dedicated, enthusiastic and selfless service, failing health dictated that she could no longer continue with her duties and responsibilities to the Manor House. Miss Forster was, by this time, living in Dorset which made it difficult for her to attend meetings and to maintain any sort of regular, personal contact with her fellow trustees. The following tribute was paid to Miss Forster and recorded in the Minute book.

"The members of the present Manor House Committee wish to record their appreciation of Miss Forster's invaluable pioneer work in the campaign to save the beautiful old half-timbered house in Solihull. She, together with Mr Thompson, Headmaster of Solihull School, and Mr John Burman, a local historian, gathered together a committee to raise the money to buy the House by public subscription and many fund raising activities. It proved to be a long and arduous campaign, but encouraged by Miss Forster's motto, "Dogged does it", was finally successful.

Miss Forster became one of the first Trustees and remained on the Committee, formed to manage and maintain the House, acting as Secretary for some years and always one of our most tireless supporters until her retirement in 1961, when she left Solihull.

She also infected the staff and pupils of her school with her enthusiasm and there still remains strong links between the Manor House and Malvern Hall, both Greswolde homes.

Solihull and the Manor House owe her a great debt, and we who are continuing the work are indeed most grateful."

Miss Forster passed away in 1981.

That was undoubtedly the most significant event of the year. Financial considerations occupied the attention of the Committee as inflation continued to impact on the provision of services, necessitating further increases in room hire charges in an attempt to balance the books. The Committee was fortunate to have Bob Garwood in charge of its finances (Honorary Treasurer from 1974 to 1988). Some very astute financial investments and skilled funds' management helped to offset the worst of the inflationary pressures and to keep the Manor House accounts in credit. Despite the upward movement in room hire charges, the Red Cross finally accepted the deal offered to them for Room 7 and signed up for a further three year licence in December. Bob reported the accounts to be "*in a healthy state*."

In September 1981 the Committee adopted a new draft Deed of Variation, drawn up by Ray Pope, then Chairman of the Manor House Committee, to update the original Trust Deed of April 1946. This document incorporated some (allegedly) relatively minor amendments and some tidying up of the practical matters associated with the running of the Charity. One of the 'minor' variations being proposed was that the Chairman, Honorary Secretary and Honorary Treasurer should all be elected by the members at the AGM of the Charity. This became increasingly controversial and although the draft Deed shuttled back and forth between the Committee and the solicitors for the Manor House for several years, it was never adopted. The election of the Committee Chairman continues to be the prerogative of the Committee at its first meeting following each AGM.

At its first meeting in 1982, the Committee approved

- a further 10% hike in room hire charges to become effective in May: and
- the dedication of Room 4 to the memory of Miss Flora Macrae Forster.

This latter item became a joint project with the staff, pupils and Old Girls' Association of Malvern Hall. A memorial fund had been launched by the School and it was decided that a significant proportion of the funds raised should be applied to assist with the decoration and furnishing of Room 4 at the Manor House, the balance to be contributed by the Manor House Committee. On November 5th 1983, the Forster Room was formally dedicated and on July 14th 1984 Mrs Barbara Kirk, Trustee, officiated at the formal opening ceremony, both events having been attended by members of Malvern Hall OGA and the Solihull Manor House Charity.

Back in 1982, the maintenance and upkeep of the gardens became too much for "Griff", who passed the baton to Dr Elisabeth Scull, her able and enthusiastic 'deputy.' In August of that same year, the Committee repaid the balance of the SMBC loan, thus finally clearing the debt incurred by the 1978 restoration programme. A further piece of tidying up was also accomplished towards the close of the year – a new front door was installed at long last. This project had lumbered on for months and months, partly because the original cost estimates were excessive and then by the failure of the appointed contractor to deliver on his promises. The final act performed by the Committee in 1982 before they 'shut the door' on another memorable year, was to commission a water colour of the Manor House by Paul Whiston. Seen as a major fund raiser selling at £25 mounted and £40 framed, the initial planned order of a limited edition of 100 prints was, wisely, reduced to 20. The last copy was finally sold at the turn of the years 1984/85 and no further order was placed.

Long and dedicated service is a theme which runs through the 20th century history of the Manor House. Had a Manor House Long Service Medal been created, Mrs Phyllis Miller, the Warden, would certainly have been qualified to receive one. She joined the Manor House team in 1952 and twenty years later in 1972, she was appointed to the post of Warden. Now in 1983, Mrs Miller intimated that she wanted to stand aside and let someone else take on the mantle. In preparation to become her successor, Mrs Lesley Lawrie was first appointed Deputy Warden in January of that year, taking over as Warden in January 1984. At a presentation on December 4th 1983, Mrs Miller received a gift of some garden furniture and a painting of the Manor House. If I have correctly interpreted the records, Mrs Miller remained as part of the team at the Manor House for a further four years, finally retiring in 1988, having completed some thirty six years of service.

Early on in my research I found a reference to a history of the Manor House which had been prepared by Ray Pope. "If only I could find that," I thought. "It would make my task so much easier." Luck was not on my side and it was not until I had reached this stage of the writing project that I finally unearthed several copies of Ray's composition. I devoured it with great interest and was absolutely amazed that we concurred on every aspect of our research into the history of the House. Ray managed to cram all his findings into four A5 pages, equivalent to the opening chapter of my work. Such concise use of words is to be admired. In my own defence, I have selected a much wider canvas upon which to draw my picture, dwelling to a greater extent on the personalities behind the scenes and elaborating on the management and running of the House against the backdrop of the historical aspects of the Manor House. Ray's work, titled "The Manor House, 126 High Street, Solihull", is dated 1.3.83. Copies are being retained in the archives for future reference.

Another significant event, although not seen as such at the time, occurred on April 11th 1983. Paul Burley, then the Honorary Architect to the Solihull Manor House Charity and a member of the Manor House Committee, chaired the meeting of the Committee held on that date, in the absence of the Chairman, Ray Pope. Paul was subsequently elected Chairman of the Committee in 1986 and has held the post ever since. In that respect, he continues the 'Kirk-Burley Dynasty', following in the footsteps of both his late father-in-law and mother-in-law, Esmond and Barbara Kirk. Collectively, they now account for some forty eight years of chairmanship out of a total of sixty two since the Charity was formed.

The Manor House by Paul Whiston (1982).

Vandalism is a recurring theme throughout 1983. Several attempted break-ins were reported and a small sum of cash, £9.33, was reported to have been stolen from the Red Cross shop on November 7th. Nine days later, the same 'suspicious young man' was back at the Manor House, this time poking about in the attic. There was some conjecture that he was looking for a hiding place to enable him to remain inside the building and then trawl through all the rooms after locking up had been completed that evening. Security was severely tightened after these incidents occurred.

I should pay tribute to the continuing hard work of the Ladies' Group on the Manor House Committee who reported having raised around £1,200 in 1983 from a series of events, coffee mornings, etc., enabling much needed decorating, re-furnishing and improvements to the garden to be carried out without being a drain on the funds of the Charity. Such activities were not, however, conducted without contention. The Ladies' Group had the audacity to open a separate bank account through which it could process its funds, a move which met with severe condemnation from Honorary Treasurer Bob Garwood. This was just another instance of the strained relationships I mentioned at the commencement of this chapter. Such was Bob's persuasive powers that the Ladies' Group succumbed to the pressure and closed its account – but not until April 1987!

Chapter Eight
1984 to 1987

In March 1984, Mrs Gill Clarke was recruited to join the small team of paid staff who helped to run the Manor House and the numerous events which were staged there. If I have followed Gill's career correctly, she went on to become Part-time Warden in 1990–91 and then Deputy Warden in 1992, a post which she has held ever since. Yet another fine example of long and dedicated service by a member of the Manor House team. Gill's husband, John, was approached to help out on a part-time basis in 2001 and continues to this day to provide support to Gill on her duty days.

August 5th of that year saw the first organised visit to the Manor House of a party comprising some forty-five members of the Griswold family, who had come over from America to visit some of the former family homes in England. They all signed the visitors' book and added some very complimentary remarks indicating just how much they had enjoyed their visit to Solihull and the Manor House in particular. This was to prove to be just the first of several such visits made in subsequent years. So far I have found reference made to visits in 1987, 1990 (two visits – June and September), 1993, 1994 and 1997.

David Patterson, a loyal and very supportive Life Subscriber to the Solihull Manor House Charity since 1975, co-ordinated these visits. In an email David sent to me on March 6th, he told me that these visits were organised by Jim and Bonnie Griswold, leading lights in The Griswold Family Association of America. Apparently, on one such visit, David gave a lecture on the history of the Greswold and Griswold families. In closing his email, David wrote, "*Over the years I have attended and enjoyed many events, meetings, courses, celebrations and partaken of many excellent lunches and coffees. For all of these the Manor House has always been a welcoming and appropriate setting. We are all enormously indebted to the present and past members of the Committee and management. Their efforts have secured the existence of this much loved building for the use and enjoyment of so many and for its contribution to the character and history of Solihull."*

Ray Pope; Rt Hon John Taylor MP; Mrs Taylor; Bill and Mrs Wall.

By the time 1984 was drawing to a close, the Honorary Treasurer was able to report that the funds of the Charity were in a much healthier state than they had been at the turn of the decade. The Honorary Architect's structural survey presented to the Committee in January 1985 listed repairs and restoration work which, if it had all been carried out at that time, would have wiped out those financial reserves. In the end, the Committee sanctioned work during 1985 which would account for around 25% of the funds of the Charity. The remainder of the work was held over until a later date.

1985 was a time for celebration. It marked the fortieth anniversary of the acquisition of the Manor House from Ansells Brewery. An Open Day was held on March 16th to mark the occasion, attended by, amongst many others, the Mayor and Mayoress, Councillor and Mrs Geoffrey Norman Gibbons. Even the foul weather could not dampen the spirits of the hosts and their guests, according to the reports made at that time.

A couple of months after this event, the Solihull Chess Club decided to decamp to the Bridge Club for all further meetings. This marked the end of a forty year association with the Manor House and as such was regarded as a sad loss by the Manor House Committee. As in most close and long-standing relationships, there had been differences between the parties from time-to-time. The most contentious issue, which cropped up again and again, was the inability of the Chess Club to meet its deadline for vacating the room it used at the House. Whilst the staff of the Manor House had a fixed finishing time for locking up the House at the end of each evening, the Chess Club members found it impossible to end their games at such a predetermined hour. On one occasion, having been left to lock up when they finished, they allegedly left without securing the House which remained open all night!

In June 1985 the Manor House Committee received an approach from a firm of Chartered Surveyors, acting on behalf of a property developer, expressing an interest in creating a row of retail units in the rear garden of the Manor House, facing on to Manor Walk. This approach came shortly after the retail units had been built on the opposite side of Manor Walk. It was suggested that the Manor House may be

Rt Hon John Taylor MP and Dr Elisabeth Scull at the Open Day celebration.

interested in leasing the land or even in an outright sale. The approach was given careful consideration and then graciously declined. Having suffered from the imposition of earlier compulsory purchase orders over tracts of land belonging to the Charity, the Committee was left with a certain amount of unease about where such an approach may go from there.

The year closed with mention at the November meeting of the Committee of the threat of litigation by the owners of Peter's Bookshop at 124 High Street, the unit adjoining the Manor House. It was alleged that the Manor House had committed an act of trespass by straying two inches over the boundary line when erecting an extension to the old storeroom at the back of the west wing of the building. The dispute was referred to the Manor House's solicitors, John Taylor & Company.

1986 opened with a serious case of vandalism which triggered a whole new debate about security of the House. On the night of January 10th, at closing time for the neighbouring Snooty Fox pub, someone broke one of the windows in the Kirk Room and then proceeded to smash the window frame. The perpetrator was arrested but not before the on-duty staff at the Manor House had been well and truly terrified.

At the April meeting of the Manor House Committee, Ray Pope, the Chairman, announced that he would not be standing for re-election following that year's AGM of the Charity. Ray had joined the Committee in 1975 and had been elected Chairman in 1977 and in each of the subsequent years. Ray had presided over several turbulent years in the life of the Manor House and obviously felt that it was time to step aside to make room for someone with new ideas and fresh enthusiasm to take the Charity forward. It would appear

Bob and Lucy Garwood.

that his decision to stand aside was greeted with anguish and concern by most of the members of the team. Presentations to Ray and his wife, Pat, were made at the May meeting of the Committee, of which Ray had decided to remain a member to provide an element of continuity during a time of change.

The Minutes of the 1986 Annual General Meeting of the Solihull Manor House Charity records, amongst other matters, the completion of a "History of the Manor House" by Ray Pope. Stella Wright, then Honorary Secretary, is credited with having prepared the manuscript for Ray. At this stage in my research project, I have, sadly, failed to unearth a copy of this work. I am still trawling through the archives so I can only hope that it turns up by the time I finish the project.

A fall off in the level of evening bookings for rooms at the Manor House around this time signalled the start of a trend which would bring about a significant change in the use to which the House would be put in the future. In anticipation of this, Paul Burley, now formally in the Chair, produced a paper entitled "Food for Thought" to provoke discussion amongst members of the Committee which might lead to the production of a new policy statement. The continuing threat of compulsory purchase of part of the land at the rear of the House, the imminent publication of detailed plans for the development of the land at the back of the High Street and the pedestrianisation of the High Street, blocking access to the Manor House car park were all factors which were creating unease in the minds of Committee members.

By the end of the year, the Committee had decided to commission a complete upgrade of the main kitchen adjacent to the Glendon Room, to convert the former ladies' toilet on the first floor into a mini kitchen and to upgrade some of the electrical wiring. The task of converting the upstairs loo was the first project to be undertaken and this was completed by the beginning of April 1987. The refurbishment of the ground floor kitchen

Barbara Kirk and Paul Burley at the 1984 Christmas Party.

was finally started in mid December 1987 and completed in February of the following year. The electrical re-wiring work ran concurrently with the kitchen refurbishment. Whether by foresight or good fortune, the enhanced kitchen facilities enabled the staff to be much more adventurous in the provision of snacks and beverages and it was not too long before it became apparent that a full time caterer would be needed to meet the ever increasing demands of visitors to the Manor House. A catering franchise was offered to and taken up by Lynne Blackmore in September 1988 and was formalised by the end of the year. At that time the Kirk Room was being used as the dining area.

Back in the closing months of 1986, the owners of Peter's Bookshop were following up on their offensive concerning the alleged act of trespass to which the Committee was turning a deaf ear, the Ladies' Group had decided to rename itself the Friends' Group and the development plans which threatened the land at the back of the Manor House were still causing considerable anxiety to everyone concerned. On a positive note, the Honorary Treasurer was able to assure the Committee that the funds were in a healthy state and that the reserves were more than adequate to meet the costs of the kitchen and rewiring upgrades.

In the middle of 1987, as a defensive move and in an attempt to ward off the possibility of the compulsory purchase of any further land belonging to the Manor House, the Committee took the battle to the Solihull Metropolitan Borough Council by proposing that the two parties should enter into a joint venture to create a museum/heritage centre in the Manor House garden. The initially enthusiastic response from SMBC quickly cooled and within six months of the initial approach, the project was dead in the water.

Meanwhile, Laura Ashley had moved in at 124 High Street as successor to Peter's Bookshop. An approach by the owners of that unit to purchase the Manor House was politely declined. There was some speculation around this time that the Manor House Charity was in financial difficulties, a rumour which perhaps triggered this approach.

In September 1987, Lesley Lawrie, the Warden resigned to take up another appointment elsewhere. A glowing tribute was paid to Lesley by the Committee in recognition of her enthusiasm and dedication throughout the four years she had been at the Manor House. A search for a successor resulted in the appointment of Jock Pickering as Temporary Warden. He was quickly confirmed in post as the Warden in the light of his aptitude and enthusiasm for the job.

The year closed on another sad note. Dr Elisabeth Scull decided to stand down as the Honorary Head Gardener in November. Although the records are silent on the exact reason for her resignation, there are some indications, when reading between the lines, that there may have been a dispute between Elisabeth and one or more members of the Committee. Dorothy Ramsay, the Vice Chairman agreed to step in to fill the vacancy in February 1988.

Chapter Nine

The End of the Eighties

1988 opened on a low note. Bob Garwood, the indispensable Honorary Treasurer, who had held the post since 1974, was seriously ill in hospital. It soon became evident that Bob would be unable to fulfil his role for some time, if at all. Ken Rule was co-opted to serve as Assistant Honorary Treasurer in Bob's absence.

Bob Garwood passed away on Easter Sunday, April 3rd, 1988. At the Committee meeting which followed his passing, Stella Wright, Honorary Secretary, paid the following tribute to Bob on behalf of the Trustees and the members of the Committee.

"To him accounts were a means to enabling good things to happen. He was always prepared to take calculated risks on our behalf, to look after our staff individually, to work with our Wardens and if necessary, train them. All these hours of work were his contribution to a well run establishment, clear in its aim of beautifying the building for future generations to admire."

At the same meeting it was resolved to name Room 2 "The Garwood Room" *"as a token of affection and thanks for Bob Garwood's work for the Manor House."* An October date was set for the actual naming ceremony to take place. In the interim, the room would undergo refurbishment and towards this end several significant donations were received from friends and admirers of the late Bob Garwood. In addition, a sum of £70 was raised from the staging of "A Midsummer Night's Dream" in the back courtyard of the Manor House by the Union Theatre company.

The Committee lost another hard working and dedicated member when Pamela May stood down on March 22nd. Pamela had joined the Committee back in January 1976, became Assistant Honorary Secretary in May of the same year, Honorary Secretary in 1977 and Vice Chairman from 1983 until 1985. As it subsequently transpired, this was not to be the end of Pamela's voluntary work for the Charity. In response to an appeal for new members to join the Committee in 2006, Pamela stepped forward and was quickly co-opted in November of that year. My task of researching the history of the Manor House has been made so much more simple thanks to Pamela's involvement. The Manor House archives had fallen into a state of some disarray and disorder in recent years. Pamela rose to the challenge to sort them into some sort of order. Whilst that project is still ongoing at the time of writing this chapter, it is evident that the end result will be a great credit to Pamela and a huge benefit to anyone else who wants to trawl through the records in the future.

Other changes in personnel in 1988 included the departure from the Committee of Ray Pope, who could not be dissuaded from resigning at that year's AGM. Ray had, by this time, served for a total of thirteen years, having been co-opted in 1975. Joining the team was Bill Stirling, a partner in the accountancy practice of Stirling & Co. Ken Rule, Bill Stirling and Martin Brown, then the auditor, had combined forces to produce a set of annual accounts following the death of Bob Garwood. Bill was co-opted to serve as Honorary Treasurer in October 1988. The transition period took a little time and it became necessary to postpone the 1988 AGM until 1989. The Charity's financial reserves proved to be sound, which was fortunate given the nature of events which would occur towards the end of 1989.

Another addition to the ranks of Committee members was Michael Mogano, then an Area Director with Lloyds Bank. He was nominated by Paul Burley and co-opted to serve on the Committee at its meeting of October 13th 1988. I mention Mike because it was him who persuaded me to join the Committee in 2005 so, in a way, he must take responsibility/blame/credit for the production of this history!

At that same Committee meeting in October, the members voted in favour of the adoption of a new draft constitution for recommendation to the Charity at a subsequent general meeting. This was the same revised constitution drafted by Ray Pope some seven years earlier. It had been back and forward to the Charity's solicitors, had undergone several redrafts and even now would still be subject to further legal redrafting before it could be implemented. This was Ray Pope's swansong.

1988 closed with the Committee still facing the same dilemma. How could they implement a change of use of the House to guarantee higher levels of income to meet ever-rising costs of maintenance, utilities and overheads? There was a need to consider how best the land could be used to fend off the threat of compulsory purchase which still lurked in the background. Should they build offices, retail units, a museum or heritage centre? There was also the need to change the pattern of use of the House to reduce the wear and tear on the structure. The move into catering was proving popular. Could this be further exploited? Events were about to resolve some of these dilemmas.

Dorothy Ramsay presented a paper at the May 1989 meeting of the Manor House Committee, inspired by the various matters referred to in the previous paragraph. Dorothy's presentation of the problems facing the Solihull Manor House Charity was both eloquent and perceptive and could not have been timelier as it transpired. Other factors were presenting themselves and impacting on the need for a review of the use of the House. At the same meeting the Committee was informed that the Red Cross would be vacating Room 7 at the end of the year. This decision had been taken after months of skirmishing between the Committee and the Red Cross over the use to which the room was being put, the need to present the Manor House in a better light, the fire hazard, not to mention the odour, presented by the storing of second hand clothing in Room 7, the insistence of the Red Cross of the need to clutter up the window facing the High Street with posters and displays and attempts by the Manor House to raise the room hire charge to a more acceptable level.

On a positive note, the Committee resolved to renew the catering franchise bestowed upon Lynne Blackmore.

Brief mention was made by Paul Burley of his concern about the oak beam forming part of the kitchen ceiling and supporting the floor of the Garwood Room above. Paul was of the view that whilst there was no immediate danger, it was a matter which would require attention in the near future.

When the Committee met again in July, it was resolved that professional guidance should be sought as to how best to respond to the Solihull Metropolitan Borough Council's Town Centre Development Plan and the impact it would have on access to the car park as a result of the pedestrianisation of the High Street, the threats to the land at the rear of the

House and so on. One indication of the pressure under which the Committee was operating was Paul Burley's offer not to stand for re-election as Chairman following the impending AGM. There was absolutely no support for such a move by the Committee members and Paul was persuaded to accept a nomination and was duly re-elected. I had to smile as I read this part of the July 1989 Minutes. Nineteen years on and I had just finished writing a Minute of the January 2008 Committee meeting which dealt with the same issue in almost identical manner. "If it aint broke, don't fix it", was the overwhelming view of the Committee.

But back then in the summer of 1989, it was "broke" and it had to be "fixed." Upon further examination, the split beam in the kitchen proved to be in a dangerous state. An examination of the beam in the Kirk Room revealed that it too was in an unsafe condition. The House was closed on August 14th out of consideration for the safety of the public and users of the building. There followed a frantic period of activity. Tenders for the urgent repair work were invited. Replacement seasoned oak beams had to be sourced. Closure notices had to be issued to all users of the House. The catering franchise was suspended. Funding for the repair work had to sourced. The initial estimate of the cost of the work was put at £25k. Although the Charity's financial reserves were sufficient to meet the cost, they would be seriously depleted and it was resolved that loans, grants or other forms of financial support should be sought.

Seasoned oak beams were imported from France. Elvins Construction Company Limited was commissioned to carry out the work. It was estimated that the House would have to remain closed until the end of the year. Some rewiring would have to be carried out as a result of the roof repairs. Jock Pickering, the Warden managed to find temporary employment for some of the House staff, thus easing the demands on the Charity's resources and keeping the staff in work.

The repair work appears to have been well planned and executed and on the 28th of November, the catering franchise was reinstated with the Glendon Room being used for seating in place of the Kirk Room. A side entry off Manor Way enabled users to access the tea room while work was still going on at the front of the House. The rewiring work had to be held over until after Christmas. The completion of this programme and the

Left: Mrs Lynne Blackmore, Tea Room proprietress. Right: One of the imported oak beams being delivered through the window of the Kirk Room.

refurbishment which followed resulted in the Manor House remaining closed until March 13th 1990.

The re-opening was reported in the local newspaper as follows:

When the first part of Solihull's historic Manor House reopened last week, the first customers were given more than they bargained for. The Tea Room closed last July after it was discovered that the Manor House was suffering from severe structural problems. Mrs Lynne Blackmore, Tea Room proprietress, has spent four months waiting for the building to be repaired. She was so delighted to be back in business that she offered desserts free of charge. Lynne offered all customers a free mince pie if they bought a hot drink on reopening day.

The threatened failure of the beams supporting the upper floor of the House was attributed to stress resulting from over use of the building, according to the structural engineer whose opinion had been sought. Although almost universally accepted by the Committee members as having been the case for some considerable time, confirmation by a qualified professional forced the issue to the top of the agenda along with an urgent need to determine the use to which the Manor House should be put in the future. The solicitors assured the Committee that a change of use to office accommodation was within the terms of the Trust Deed. Rooms 3, 4 and 5 were put under short-term licence to Sterling Management Consultants and the Glendon Room was allocated to Lynne Blackmore as part of the catering franchise. In parallel with this, the Committee gave consideration to leasing the Manor House to SMBC for use as an arts/heritage/history centre. There was less than enthusiastic support for this latter idea.

So the eighties ended on a troubled note. There were lots of unanswered questions about the future management and use of the House; grave concerns over the plans for the new shopping complex and the pedestrianisation of the High Street; and some anxiety about the rather precarious financial position of the Charity after it had settled the bills for the structural and rewiring work. The situation was set out succinctly by Stella Wright, the Honorary Secretary, in a paper dated December 5th 1989, entitled "Policy Document for Manor House – December 1989."

Stresses and strains were evident between Trustees, Committee members, users and the community at large. This was probably the biggest crisis to confront the Charity since it had taken over the Manor House from Ansells Brewery in 1946.

Chapter Ten

1990 to 1991

The new decade opened on the same low note as had been sounding at the end of the eighties but for a very different reason. Jock Pickering, the Warden, had suffered a heart attack at the beginning of January and was lying seriously ill in hospital when the Committee met for the first time that year, on February 15th. It was clear that Jock would never return to take up his duties. When he passed away on March 7th, tributes flowed in, including the one recorded in the Minute Book by Stella Wright the Honorary Secretary.

"Mrs Wright said Jock was badly missed during the weeks of his illness and it was sad he would not be there to re-open the House on March 13th. Jock had been an inspiration to work with; young at heart, professional and with a great love of the House. He always looked to the future and the possibility of happier times which he was sure could be achieved."

Running in parallel with this tragedy was the works programme to complete the upgrading of the electrical circuitry and the redecorations following the replacement of the faulty oak beams in the old kitchen and the Kirk Room. It was beginning to be evident that the final bill for all of this work would not be far short of £30k, which would severely deplete the financial reserves of the Charity. No grants or any form of financial assistance was forthcoming.

The Committee examined several options open to them to safeguard the future of the Charity and the Manor House, including the transfer of the freehold of the House and land to SMBC in exchange for the creation of a heritage centre development on the site, as an appendage to the House. These discussions were set to rumble on for several months until at last the Committee lost patience with the Council and withdrew from any further negotiations in October of that year. When the Council made a fresh approach to the Committee in January of 1991 with an alternative proposal for the development of some ground at the rear of the House, the Committee wasted little time in rejecting it. It was around that time that the town centre development company had gone into liquidation, so there was a lot of uncertainty surrounding the SMBC's own plans for the future.

The recruitment of a new Warden to replace Jock Pickering was briefly considered in the spring of 1990 but as the income was inadequate to pay for such a service, the subject was put on the back burner and it was left to the Committee, primarily the Vice Chairman, Dorothy Ramsay and the Honorary Treasurer, Stella Wright to fill the gap.

The House re-opened on March 13th 1990 as planned. Lynne Blackmore was by this time well established as the catering franchisee in the Glendon Room and she was shortly to be joined by Sterling Management Consultants in Rooms 3, 4 and 5. By the middle of the year it was reported that bookings were on the increase, the tea room was getting busier and the gardens were in good shape. The autumn of 1990 brought about an economic downturn which had an adverse effect on the community at large and upon the Manor House in particular, where the finances were already in a parlous state. Sterling Management gave notice that it would be quitting its rooms at the end of the year, but that it wished to retain an option to return when the economy picked up again, for which it was happy to pay a fee.

Lynne Blackmore intimated that she would be willing to renew the licence on the kitchen and Glendon Room for a further period of three years from January 1st 1991, so this gave the Committee a small ray of hope for the future.

In the background, the list of repair and maintenance jobs was growing ever longer but there was little which could be done about it as there were no funds available to commission such work.

A decision to seek a licensee for Room 6 was passed by the Committee, with some reservations, and by April 1st 1991, Wilfrid Rogers, Consulting Engineer had moved in. Another steady source of income which would help to stabilise the finances. But far more would be needed before the Committee could begin to see a secure future for the Charity. A deficit budget had been presented to the Committee for consideration by the

Honorary Treasurer, Martin Brown. Mike Mogano, a member of the Committee, spoke against the adoption of such a budget and persuaded the Committee to revise its thinking and to set a higher target for income from the casual hiring of the rooms at the House. And so a planned deficit was converted into a projected surplus.

This appears to have been a pivotal point which resulted in the production of a new mission statement set out in a 'Policy Discussion Paper: June 1991', prepared by Paul Burley, the Chairman, and tabled for discussion by the Committee when it met on July 9th 1991. The content was perceptive, far-sighted, clearly set out and demanding of the total support of the entire Committee to secure the future of the Manor House and the Solihull Manor House Charity. Here are just one or two paragraphs taken from that document:

"In the past we have tried to maximise our income from lettings which has resulted in an over-use of the House. The use by classes, charities and societies, resulted in extensive wear and tear on the fabric of the House, over extended our management resources and generated limited income which was out of all proportion to the effort involved.

It is no longer possible to generate the income we need, solely from occasional lettings, due largely to an over provision of subsidised facilities elsewhere."

And:

"Our future policy could be to create a sensible balance between income from permanent lettings and income from the hire of rooms for use by the local community. We need to attract more 'upmarket' users and we will need to improve furnishings and facilities in the House, particularly the Garwood Room.

Under a section headed 'Management', there is a paragraph which runs as follows:

"In recent years there has been a lack of unity within the Committee, and we have now reached the point where Committee meetings are largely a waste of time. Matters which have been discussed and voted on in previous meetings are continually resurrected. We therefore need to restructure the Committee by accepting resignations from those who have not been able to accept majority decisions. Unless this restructuring takes place the present Officers intend submitting their resignations at the next AGM in October."

If ever there was a time for strong leadership it was then and Paul Burley rose to the challenge. Gillian Clarke who was appointed Part Time Warden in

1990 and had been on the payroll since 1984, resigned her post earlier in 1991 because she had become unsettled by the divisions existing between some of the members of the Committee, described at the time as being *"a divided and acrimonious situation."*

The Chairman was intent upon resolving the situation and demanded unanimous support for the policies set out in the above discussion document. The Honorary Treasurer, Bill Stirling, was unable to give that support and was relieved of his position. Although Bill was a relative newcomer to the Committee, he had made a significant contribution by taking on the mantle following the death of Bob Garwood. Mrs Whyte *"resigned from the Committee and left the meeting"*, ending an unbroken period of dedicated service which commenced in the early seventies. Gladys Creed and Ron Simmons tendered their resignations following that crucial meeting. Both had given many years of loyal and dedicated service to the Committee but obviously felt that it was now time to step aside and let someone else carry on the struggle. And so a further turning point in the management, policy and running of the House had been reached, with Paul Burley exerting his authority to force through the new agenda.

Ron and Gladys Simmons who, collectively, had served on the Committee for seventeen years, are still active supporters of and Life Subscribers to the Solihull Manor House Charity. Gladys recalled, in response to my request for anecdotal memories, that, *"Ron worked in the Manor House garden for many years"* and *"also attended Beekeepers' meetings"* whilst she, *"attended flower arranging classes"* and along with her husband, *"attended Solihull Horticultural meetings."* Gladys, *"also hired the rooms for the charity coffee mornings."*

At the following Committee meeting, held on September 11th 1991, the new Policy Document received the unanimous support of the members. Martin Brown, formerly the Charity's auditor, and latterly the Assistant Treasurer, was elected to serve as Honorary Treasurer until the next AGM of the Charity. The appointment of a House Manager on July 15th was announced. Michael Styles had been selected from a short list of candidates to fulfil the duties of the former Warden.

The year closed to mixed reviews. A valuable picture, a still life of fruit by Vincent Clare, had been stolen from the Garwood Room early in October; Mr

Styles, the new House Manager was not measuring up; a six month licence had been granted to Paul Kitson, Osteopath in respect of the old Storeroom; and the 200 Club, a fund raising idea created by Martin Brown, was launched. The year-end results showed a small surplus of income over expenditure, largely due to an upturn in casual lettings, but the finances of the Charity were still in a precarious position. Hidden amongst all these domestic matters which troubled the Committee was the fact that the Manor House had turned a corner. The scene had been set for a much brighter future, although it had may not have been realised by the Manor House Committee at that time. The Manor House we see and love today, is the result of the vision which was created by Paul Burley and his team back there in 1991.

Chapter Eleven

1992 to 1995

The 200 Club, the brainchild of Martin Brown, was a local lottery. For an annual subscription of £1 (still that amount to this day) one lucky member stood to win £50 every month or the top prize of £500, drawn in December each year. Any surplus funds, after paying out the prize money, would be donated to The Solihull Manor House Charity to go towards the upkeep of the Manor House. The idea caught on and by the end of the first year, 1992, 170 members had enrolled. Since then numbers have, from time to time, climbed up to the mid 200's and dipped down at other times to between 100 and 150. It is a most attractive way of giving to Charity, whilst standing the chance of recouping any donation made. Such inventiveness, and dedication to his role as Honorary Treasurer, was typical of Martin Brown.

The Committee's new strategy of trying to find companies to occupy some of the rooms at the Manor House on short term licences was beginning to pay off by the end of 1992. Polly Jones Associates, a small firm of table-top publishers, had taken a three year licence on the Forster Room in the summer and Mr Steven Beetison, an independent financial adviser, was occupying Room 7 (the old Red Cross room) on a one year licence starting that autumn. Sadly, Polly Jones Associates had to be released from its obligations as the electrical demands being placed upon the circuitry in the Forster Room were excessive and in danger of causing a fire in the House.

Commercial development of part of the Manor House garden was again under consideration but the plans for a small community development fronting on to Manor Walk were rejected by SMBC in August of 1993. The Touchwood development plan had been reactivated by a new firm appointed to succeed the company which had gone into liquidation. Once again, the Committee was expressing concern about access to the car park at the Manor House and it was seeking assurances from SMBC that there would be adequate provision made once the old municipal car park disappeared.

A small start was being made to catch up on the backlog of maintenance work which had accumulated during and immediately after the enforced closure of the House. The exterior of the building had been painted and some minor roof repairs and joinery work carried out by the close of 1992.

At its October meeting that year, the Committee decided to dedicate Room 3 to the memory of Jock Pickering by naming it the Pickering Room. Jock's widow, Gladys, was invited to perform the naming ceremony on February 13th 1993.

Perhaps the most significant event in 1992 was the recruitment of a new Warden. It was to be out with one Michael and in with another Michael. Michael Styles tendered his resignation with effect from the end of July and Michael Zimmerman, the current Warden, was recruited to fill the vacancy. A bonus was that Gill Clarke agreed to return and job-share with Michael Zimmerman. After a short settling-in period, Gill elected to become Deputy Warden while Michael Zimmerman took on the mantle of Warden. This proved to be a winning formula which still obtains at the date of compiling this part of the story (February 2008).

Just before the Committee met on February 23rd 1993, Stella Wright submitted her resignation as Honorary Secretary, this to take immediate effect. As was reported in the minutes of the meeting *"The Committee were (sic) unanimous in their gratitude for her sterling work."* In the absence of any other nomination to fill the vacancy, Martin Brown agreed to add the role of Acting Honorary Secretary to his job as Honorary Treasurer. Although this bundling-up of jobs was not universally popular with all members of the Committee, it was set to continue for the foreseeable future as no other nominee came forward.

One of Stella's last acts was the compilation of yet another Deed of Variation to amend and update the Trust Deed drawn up in 1946. The new document was discussed at the meeting of the Committee held on April 1st, again in July and yet again in August prior to its submission to and approval by the Charity Commission in September 1993. Its adoption had been

An early phase in the creation of the Manor House Garden.

approved at that year's AGM and it was finally signed off by the Committee on November 16th 1993. Anthony Collins & Company had acted throughout as solicitors to The Solihull Manor House Charity.

Yet further progress was made in 1993 with the transfer of rooms from casual use by countless community organisations to occupancy by companies, securing a steady flow of income whilst drastically reducing the footfall in the old House. Lynne Blackmore intimated in the spring of that year that she would be exercising her option to renew her licence on the kitchen and Glendon Room for a further two years with effect from January 1st 1994. Sadly this was not to be the case as Lynne withdrew that offer in the autumn, saying that she would be vacating on December 31st 1993. The search for a successor produced a lengthy list of contenders, including Druckers. A short-list was drawn up prior to final interviews being held in October from which John Banks Catering emerged as the selected candidate. As John and his team has been at the Manor House ever since and does an excellent job, this was clearly a bit of inspired selection by the interviewing panel. John Banks took over on January 15th 1994.

Elsewhere in the House in 1993, The Drives Constructed Company Limited took a licence on Room 10 for an initial period of one year with effect from May 1st; Wilfrid Rogers was still in occupancy of Room 6; and Steven Beetison had extended his licence on Room 7. Sterling Management continued to pay a retainer on Rooms 3, 4 and 5, which entitled it to use a couple of parking spaces. The new policy was beginning to pay dividends and with the rather more secure inflow of funds, the Committee was able to sanction a scheme for upgrading the Manor House gardens which had been drawn up by Margaret Hathway Tibbs, Dorothy Ramsay and Michael Zimmerman. This was to be the first step in creating the beautiful gardens with which we are familiar today.

1994 started on a tragic note. Barbara Kirk passed away in January having given a lifetime of dedicated service to the Manor House. Barbara first joined the Committee in 1949 so she had notched up forty four years of continuous service during which time she had also served as Chairman (1963 to 1977) and as a Trustee (1976 to the time of her passing). At their meeting on March 10th, the Committee observed a minute's silence. As a special tribute to her memory a bench, bearing a plaque recording her name and life span, was installed in the Manor House garden. Mrs Dorothy Ramsay was elected to fill the vacant Trustee post left by the passing of Mrs Kirk.

1994 was also the year in which the High Street was (finally) pedestrianised. Although some disruption was expected, very little was actually realised. The Committee had expressed an interest in planting a row of lime trees in front of the House as part of the scheme but its input proved to be unnecessary as the SMBC took the job on board and did the work itself.

The list of commercial occupants of rooms at the Manor House was augmented in 1994 by the arrival of Simeon Jacobs, a consulting engineer (of whom more will be said later) who took a one year licence on Room 5. Wilfrid Rogers (Room 6) agreed to a further one year extension and John Banks Catering, now well settled in, expressed its confidence in the future by requesting a three year extension of its licence covering the kitchen and Glendon Room.

Left: Solihull's Best Kept Secret! Right: Margaret Hathway Tibbs in December 1995.

With the finances now moving into a rather more settled and secure phase, the Committee was, once again, able to tackle some of the repair and maintenance tasks which had been backing up. During 1995 these were just some of the projects undertaken: repairs to the fire escape leading from the Garwood Room; the laying of a new carpet in Room 6; replacement guttering on the Manor Walk side of the House; the replacement of some roof tiles; stage three of an ongoing upgrade to the electrics; fitting of eight new sash windows to the front of the House; the provision of new garden gates; and the redecoration of the Kirk Room. During the preparatory work for this last project, a fireplace was 'discovered', subsequently restored and finally fitted with a suitable stove, which is still there today.

One of the highlights of 1995 was the staging of the inaugural Rare Plant Sale in the Manor House gardens. The idea was the brainchild of Margaret Hathway Tibbs and Dorothy Ramsay. First mooted back in the autumn of 1994 as a fund-raising project, it took off and, when held on May 14th 1995, was a huge success, attended by the Mayor and local MP John Taylor.

The annual licensee review held in November 1995 threw up very few changes. The only departure was Simeon Jacobs. David Greening was moving from Room 10 to Room 5 where Sim had been and a new licensee, Gail Sparkes had agreed to take over Room 10 for a minimum of thirteen months from December 1995.

The only cloud upon the horizon at this time was the compulsory purchase order ("CPO") which had been served upon the Charity by the SMBC as part of the Touchwood development programme. The minutes of the meetings are less than specific as to the extent of the land under threat by the CPO but one assumes that it covered the rear and western boundaries of the gardens which abutted the proposed Touchwood Shopping Centre. A public enquiry had been scheduled for January 1996, at which the Solihull Manor House Charity would be represented.

Chapter Twelve

1996 to 1998

Amazingly, for the first time in the compilation of this short history of the Manor House, there is very little of any significance to report for a whole year, in this case, 1996, other than the recruitment of Councillor Honor Cox to the ranks of the Committee. What is remarkable about Honor joining the Committee is the fact that she was following in the footsteps of her father, Councillor George Carter. Councillor Carter appears to have been co-opted to serve around 1956 and can be traced through to 1973. Honor, who is still on the Committee (2008) is, therefore, well on the way to matching her father's seventeen year period of dedicated service.

Michael Zimmerman; Dorothy Ramsay; Martin Brown.

It was even a relatively quiet year on the maintenance and repairs front, with the exception of the laying of a new floor in the Glendon Room. As further revelations will show, this turned out to be an inopportune investment. Even the Rare Plant Sale organised in 1996 proved to be quiet and the exercise was never repeated. All was relatively settled on the licensee front too, with the only change being the departure of Gail Sparkes from the old Store Room, which was then taken over by John Banks Catering as an office.

If 1996 was a quiet year, 1997 was set to make up for it. The first news to stun the Committee when it met on January 23rd, was of the passing away early in January of Bill Wall, then 102 years old. The Committee stood for a minute in silent tribute to Bill. He would be missed. No longer would there be calls from Bill to make provision for a resident warden. Despite there being no support for this idea and the fact that it was totally impractical, Bill would always put it forward whenever the subject of security of the House came up for discussion. But I must not make light of his enormous contribution to the work of The Solihull Manor House Charity. Councillor Wall was Honorary Treasurer from 1948 until he was elected Mayor of the Burgh in 1961. After one year of enforced absence to attend to his Mayoral duties, Bill rejoined the Committee in 1962 and became a Trustee in 1976, both of which roles he more than adequately fulfilled until his death at the beginning of 1997.

The subject of a suitable memorial to Bill took some time to resolve. First, there was to be a plaque in the House; then the Council became involved and it was decided to plant a pear tree in the Manor House garden; but then Bill's daughter, Daphne, offered to provide an armillary sphere which would be mounted on a pedestal with a suitable plaque attached, in the Manor House garden. Sadly, the original sphere was stolen and the replacement was vandalised twice.

Also at the January meeting of the Committee, the provisional accounts for 1996 were discussed and it was shown that the results were encouraging. Projects to be undertaken later in the year included yet more upgrading to the electrical wiring (later said to be due to the poor work of previous contractors) and the laying of a wooden floor in the main hall on top of the existing quarry tiles. This latter project, undertaken by Michael Zimmerman, was completed in June of that year. In the background, the CPO threat still hung over the land at the rear of the House, but with the Touchwood project being subjected to a one year delay, it was no longer imminent.

An Extraordinary Meeting had to be called in early March 1997, when it became clear that there was a conflict of interest between the terms of the Charity's Trust Deed and the remuneration terms agreed with Martin Brown and the payment of fees to S. T. Walker & Partners, Paul Burley's architectural practice. As a means of resolving the former, Martin Brown resigned as Honorary Treasurer, Acting Honorary Secretary and as a member of the Committee and was retained as Clerk to the Trustees. The S. T. Walker & Partners position was more complex and whilst it was being resolved it was deemed to be inappropriate to nominate Paul as a Trustee to fill the vacancy left by the death of Bill Wall. Anthony Collins, Solicitors, was instructed to draft a further Deed of Variation to the Trust Deed and to liaise with the Charity Commission over the wording and implementation. The draft document, which had already received the Charity Commission's tacit approval, was presented to and adopted by the 1997 AGM of the Charity and finally implemented on November 25th of that

The front of the Manor House – Britain in Bloom 1997.

year. Also at the AGM, Paul Burley was appointed to fill the vacant post of Trustee and Dorothy Ramsay was elected as the Honorary Secretary 'retrospectively', in order to comply with the terms of the original Trust Deed. Martin Brown appears to have been left to fulfil the role of Honorary Treasurer under the guise of Clerk to the Trustees.

Whilst all this was going on, there had been a bit of a splurge on repairs and maintenance. At the end of the first quarter, Martin Brown was reported to have expressed serious concern about the fact that the entire year's budgeted allocation for such work had already been exhausted. This was a concern repeated at the half-year point. This is a problem which resonates with me as it is one with which the present Committee is frequently confronted. This lovely old House demands a lot of time and attention, both of which seem to cost a lot of money!

The situation as regards licensees appears to have been pretty stable in 1997. A new addition, worthy of special mention, as she is still a licensee today (2008), is the conversion of Megan Pierce, trading as Scent to Go, from a casual user of the House to the licensee of Room 7, which she occupied with effect from January 1st 1998. It was a real pleasure to renew my acquaintanceship with Megan when I joined the Committee in 2005. We had been colleagues at the National Exhibition Centre in the seventies/eighties so we had a bit of reminiscing to do. As Megan will tell you, she can walk on water, but that's another story!

Rear Courtyard – Britain in Bloom, 1997.

1997 closed with continuing indecision about the implementation date for the start of the Touchwood development.

State interference in everyday business life was beginning to rear its ugly head around the beginning of 1998. The dreaded health and safety legislation with which all businesses now have to contend had started to creep insidiously into everyday life. The Manor House Committee, anxious to comply with such obligations, had been trying to send Michael Zimmerman on a refresher Red Cross course for many months. He finally succumbed to the pressure in the spring of that year and then followed up by sending one or two more members of the Manor House staff on a similar course and persuading John Banks to do the same. The First Aid box was checked and brought up to standard as were the emergency procedures for the safety of those persons using the House. Alarm systems and security devices became regular topics on the Committee agendas. Upgrading of electrical circuitry to meet the ever higher standards became an expensive item on the annual accounts of the Charity. How did they manage back in 1485, one wonders, with open hearths, oil lamps and naked candles, not to mention sanitation or the lack of it?

A start date for the Touchwood development was announced in the spring of 1998. January 25th 1999 saw the project get off the ground, or more accurately, begin to dig into the ground. In the meantime, battle was joined by the Committee and SMBC in an endeavour to protect access to the rear of the premises throughout the development period, ward off any encroachment on to Manor House land and to secure an appropriate sum in compensation for any inconvenience suffered or damage done to the House and gardens. A plan was issued by SMBC to show all High Street property owners/occupiers the access arrangements which would obtain throughout the development. A copy of this plan is attached to the Minutes of the Committee meeting held on March 25th 1999. It offered some reassurance to the Committee as regards access to the car park.

Judy Brown and Dorothy Ramsay.

As it transpired, Touchwood had very little adverse impact on the Manor House, although there were some fluctuations in trading patterns affecting the tea room and Scent to Go, the removal of a couple of trees and the trimming of another, the removal of the wrought iron gates giving access to the car park which were saved for re-use once the new rear wall had been constructed and some vandalism during the period when the rear of the premises was open to all comers. By October of 2000, an opening date of September 2001 for Touchwood was being trailed and the rest is history.

But I'm rushing ahead to the start of the next century and I haven't finished with this one. Back in the early part of 1998, the '97 year-end accounts showed a small surplus and the Charity's reserves were being slowly restored to afford some protection against any future catastrophe. Sadly, one source of regular income from the casual use of a room in the House was set to disappear. The Job Club, a long-time user of the House, intimated that it would be leaving as its support funding had been withdrawn. On the plus side, Sim Jacobs returned expressing an interest in taking a licence on Room 4.

When the Committee met on April 30th, it was appraised of the resignation of Committee member Alan Arnison who had then given five years of service. It also decided to rename the old kitchen 'The Griffiths

Room' as a tribute to Miss Joyce Evelyn Griffiths, who had passed away in the spring. Just as Miss Griffiths was known as Griff, so the room named in her honour would always be The Griff Room. Griff had joined the Committee in 1962 as Assistant Honorary Secretary, she became Joint Honorary Secretary in 1963 and Honorary Secretary in 1977 through until 1987. In addition, Griff was appointed as one of the Trustees of The Solihull Manor House Charity in 1980, a position she held until her passing. By my calculation, that was thirty-six years of loyal and dedicated service to the Charity. Well done, Griff. The Griff Room was formally endowed on June 28th 1998.

Within days of that event, the Committee was reeling under the weight of more bad news. Martin Brown had suffered a fatal heart attack. An emergency meeting was called on July 17th to sort out the Charity's affairs in the light of this event. Martin had made himself an invaluable asset to the Charity since he had joined the Committee in 1990. The day-to-day running and routine of the House revolved around him. Michael Zimmerman recalls that Martin visited the House at least once every day. There was a sense of great loss and of sadness. Emergency measures had to be put in place immediately, although everyone was still adjusting to the news.

- Millie Mills would be approached and invited to become Honorary Treasurer;
- Michael Zimmerman agreed to take over the day-to-day running of the office;
- Elaine Stephens agreed to do the secretarial work; and
- Judy, Martin's widow, said that she wanted to take over the running of The Manor House 200 Club.

And so the troops rallied again to bring a tragic year to a close.

A bench with an inscribed plaque was installed in the Manor House garden in the following year, as a memorial to the remarkable Martin Brown.

Chapter Thirteen

The Close of the 20th Century

When the Manor House Committee met on January 19th 1999, it co-opted David Greening to serve as Honorary Treasurer. David's appointment was scheduled to be the shortest in the history of The Solihull Manor House Charity's existence. Having had time to reflect upon the appointment by the time it met again on March 25th, the Committee asked David to withdraw from the appointment, which he duly did. It had been deemed inappropriate for a licensee to have privileged access to information about other licensees within the House. At its meeting on May 26th, the Committee co-opted Millie Mills to fill this vacancy. Millie had already prepared the 1998 accounts following the death of Martin Brown, so she had a working knowledge of what was involved. Millie continues to serve the Charity in this capacity today (2008).

At the May meeting, the Committee also co-opted Elaine Stephens to fill the vacancy for an Honorary Secretary. In truth, Elaine had been Hon Sec in all but name for some time as she had been a regular attendee at meetings of the Committee, had prepared the Minutes and undertaken much of the secretarial work. In a further effort to strengthen the Committee, Sim Jacobs was co-opted to serve at the January meeting and made his first appearance at the March meeting. This was to prove a most opportune appointment in the light of future events.

On the licensee front, everything was relatively stable at this time. The revenue flow from this quarter had been further strengthened by the granting of a licence to Mrs Anne Hammond, a residential lettings consultant, in respect of Room 3, The Pickering Room, for a period of three years. There may have been a few ripples on the surface, as a Tenants' Group was formed in mid 1999, which made representations to the Committee about some minor matters which were causing concern. Perhaps the management had taken its eye off the ball during all the turmoil of Touchwood, the passing of Martin Brown and the constant struggle to maintain the House in good order. Everything appears to have been quickly sorted out and calm was soon restored.

By granting licences on all but the Garwood, Forster, Kirk and Griff rooms, which had been retained for casual or regular short term bookings by community groups and others, the Committee had achieved a much better balance with regard to the use of and footfall through the House. The revenue flow achieved was just keeping ahead of the running and maintenance costs, enabling the Committee to put a small amount into a 'sinking' fund each year, as an 'insurance policy' against any future major renovations or repair work.

At this point, there was a great temptation for me to carry on with this story up to the present day but, at the outset, I had promised myself that I would cover the period 1900 to 2000 and I decided to do just that. I will, however, scramble just a little bit over the edge into the next century in order to complete one facet of the story which began in 1999 but did not end until 2004. It became known as 'Project 2000.' At the Committee meeting of October 7th 1999, Paul Burley floated the suggestion that an extension to the rear of the east wing (Glendon Room) should, perhaps, be considered. The Heritage Lottery Fund ("HLF") had come into being and offered itself as a source of financial support for such projects.

That was all that was Minuted. The Committee then went on to receive the resignation (retirement) of Brenda Downing who had completed 20 years of dedicated and supportive service to the Charity. A presentation to Brenda was made at that year's Christmas party, in recognition of *"her sterling work over the years."*

The east wing extension project quickly gathered momentum. In April of 2000, Paul's drawings and plans were favourably received by the Committee, with some minor amendments, and these were then submitted to SMBC in June along with the requisite planning application. Upon receiving news that SMBC was inclined to approve the planning application, an approach for funding assistance was submitted to the HLF. By June of 2001, a formal application pack had been received from HLF. Sim Jacobs, who was, a little later, to become a Trustee of the Charity, was appointed Principal Officer for the project in the documentation when it was formally submitted to HLF for its final approval. At the Committee meeting held on March 28th 2003, it was announced that a grant equal to 75% of the total cost of Project 2000 had been made by HLF. A draft timetable for the completion of the programme was drawn up and by November of that year, tenders had been invited and contractors appointed. Project 2000, costing just under £400k, commenced on April 19th 2004 and was completed on schedule and within budget on November 10th.

The west wing of the House had been totally transformed. A splendid new tea room with servery area and male, female and disabled toilet facilities had replaced the former kitchen and Glendon Room. Access from Manor Walk had been incorporated into the design, enabling visitors to reach the tea room without coming through the House. The new tea room was to prove to be very popular with Solihull residents and would prove to be an enormous financial asset too. Credit for the concept must be given to a few willing volunteers who decided to serve teas and coffees to the residents of Solihull way back in the eighties. Lynne Blackmore must also take some credit for having developed the format and for passing on the baton to John Banks who picked it up so willingly and carried it to the finishing line.

The new tea room called, most appropriately, The Burley Room, was formally opened by centenarian Molly Bullock, on December 12th 2004.

The Manor House's emergence into the 21st century had got off on a very positive note indeed. Let us all hope that it is a good omen for the future of this charming and atmospheric old House.

Solihull Community Association Affiliated Organisations as at 1949–50

Society of Arts
Beekeepers' Association
Blossomfield Club
Blythe Players
Boy Scouts Parents' Association
British Legion
British Red Cross Society – Detachment 50
British Red Cross Society – Detachment 510
Chess Club
Communist Party
Conservative and Unionist Association
Young Conservative and Unionist Association
Cricket and Tennis Club
Girl Guides Parents' Association
Girls' Training Corps
High School for Girls Parents' Association
High School for Girls Old Girls' Association
Home Guard Association
Labour Party – Elmdon Heath
Solihull Constituency Labour Party
Labour Party League of Youth
Liberal Association
Manor House Committee

Monday Club
Photographic Society
Presbyterian Church of England
Psychology Fellowship
Queen Elizabeth Hospital Linen League
Radio (Amateur) Society
Residents' Association
Rotary Club
Royal Air Force Association
Seventeen Plus Club
Swimming Club
Tenants' Association
Toc H
Toc H Women's Section
Trade – Chamber of
United Nations Association
William and Mary Rest and Recreation Society
Women's Institute

Appendix Two

Some of the Users of the Manor House in 1976

Action for Epilepsy – Solihull Group
Action Research Limited
Alpha (UK) Research Limited
Altrusa Club of Birmingham and District
Beekeepers' Association
B.J.M. Research Partners
Britannic Assurance Company Limited
British Market Research Bureau Limited
Communication Research Limited
Consumer Research Bureau
Darley Mead Court (Management) Limited
Data Sciences International Limited
Federation of Master Builders – Solihull Branch
Ffestiniog Railway Society – Midland Group
Historical Association – Mid-Warwickshire Branch
Hollymoor Hospital
Household Product Research Limited
Institution of Works Managers – Solihull Branch
Loyal Order of Moose, Sheldon Lodge No. 270
Malvern Hall Parents' Association
Metropolitan Borough of Solihull Education Committee
Midland Societies for the Blind
Muscular Dystrophy Group of Great Britain

National Association of Widows
National Westminster Group Pensioners' Association
Research Bureau Limited
Rotaract Club of Solihull
Save the Children – Solihull Branch
Sharmanians
Shirley and District Referees' Association
Shirley Friends of St Christopher's Home
Society of Spiritualists
Solihull and District Orchid Society
Solihull Area Chemist Contractors' Committee
Solihull Business and Professional Women's Club
Solihull Chess Club
Solihull Divisional Liberal Association
Solihull Horticultural Society
Solihull Society for Mentally Handicapped Children
Solihull Society of Arts – Art Section
Solihull Society of Arts – Connoisseurs' Circle
Solihull Society of Arts – Discussion Circle
Solihull Swimming and Water Polo Club
Solihull Young Liberals
St Mary's Church Bazaar Committee – Hobs Moat
The Friends of the Samaritans of Solihull
The Inner Wheel Club of Solihull
The Institute of Packaging
The National Farmers' Union
The National Trust
The Norfolk Society for Birmingham and the Midlands
The Numeriques
The Solihull Photographic Society – Cinè Group
The Sue Ryder Foundation
Toc H – Solihull Branch
Warwickshire Bridle Path Group
Yoga Classes

Appendix Three

Floor Plans of the Manor House

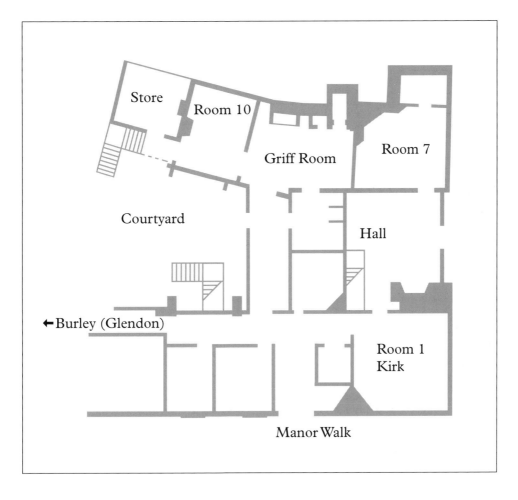

Ground Floor layout – not to scale – prepared by F Ritchie, Feb 2008.

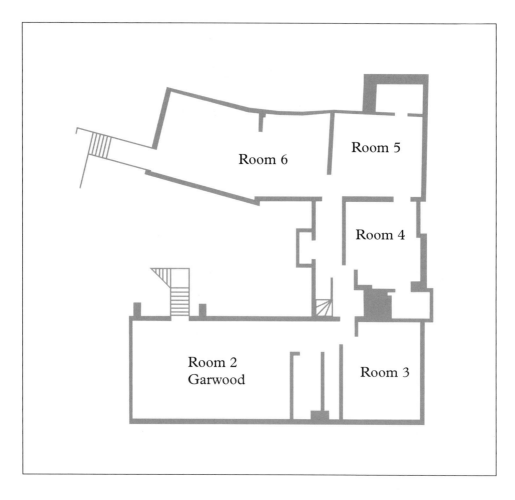

First Floor layout – not to scale – prepared by F Ritchie, Feb 2008.

Listing of Trustees and Officers of the Solihull Manor House Charity

TRUSTEES

Sir Robert Bland Bird	1946–1950
Paul Nicholas Burley	1997–Present
John P. Burman	1946–1950
Flora MacRae Forster	1946–1980
Joyce E. Griffiths	1980–1998
Mary Violet Lloyd Hampton	1951–
Simeon P. Jacobs	2001–2006
Oliver Esmond Kirk	1958–1963
Barbara Kirk	1976–1993
Roland Charles Lines	1946–1962; and
	1976–2000
Dorothy Ramsay	1994–Present
Jeremy Charles Rose	2006–Present
John William Wall	1976–1997
Dr E. St John Whitehouse	1951–1957

CHAIRMEN

1946–1947	John P. Burman
1947–1949	
1949–1951	A. Dando
1951–1963	Oliver Esmond Kirk
1963–1977	Barbara Kirk

CHAIRMEN (Continued)
1977–1986   Raymond Charles Pope
1986–Present   Paul Nicholas Burley

HONORARY SECRETARIES
1946–1969   Flora MacRae Forster
1969–1977   June Hale
1977–1985   Pamela May
1985–1993   Stella Wright
1993–1997   Martin Brown
1997–1999   Dorothy Ramsay
1999–2004   Elaine Stephens
2004–2006   Heather Scott
2006–Present   Fred Ritchie

HONORARY TREASURERS
1946–1947   Alfred Ross Thompson
1947–1948   John Rowe
1948–1961   John William Wall
1961–1964   C. Alec Clegg
1964–1974   Eric Dinwiddie
1974–1988   Robert O. Garwood
1988–1991   William Stirling
1991–1999   Martin Brown
1999–1999   David Greening
1999–Present   Beryl (Millie) Mills

Appendix Five

Map showing Land lost to Compulsory Purchase in 1962

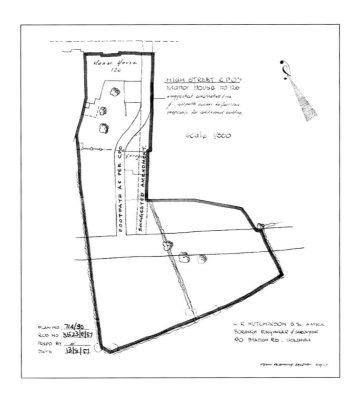

Before.... This map shows the land belonging to The Solihull Manor House Charity prior to the application of the compulsory purchase order by Solihull Borough Council, concluded in 1962, when it acquired land to create a Municipal car park at the rear of the properties fronting on to the High Street.

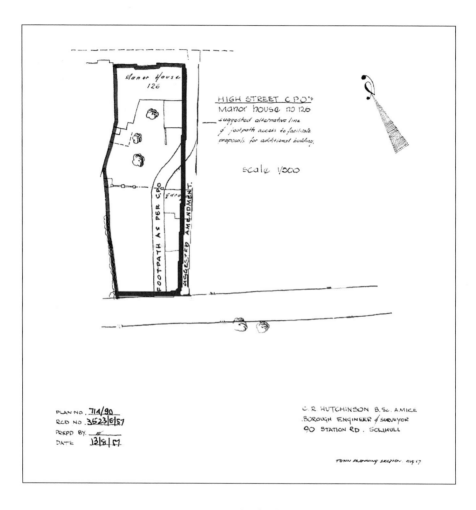

.... and after!